Music
Money
& You
Managing the Business

by Greta Pope

Greta Pope Entertainment
Chicago, Illinois

Music, Money and You!...Managing the Business
©2010 by Greta Pope Entertainment

ISBN-10: 0615383939
ISBN-13: 978-0615383934

LIBRARY OF CONGRESS CONTROL NUMBER: 2010936742

Cover design: Barron Steward of www.barronsteward.com
Interior Book Design: Lissa Woodson of www.macrompg.com

Distributed by Ingram Book Group

Greta Pope Entertainment trade paperback edition September 2010

10   9   8   7   6   5   4   3   2   1

Manufactured and Printed in the United States of America

For information regarding discounts for bulk purchases, please contact us at greta@gretapope.com.

Many thanks to Ed, Edward, Ehryck, Barron, Lissa, Margaret and Bill, without whom this book would not have been possible.

Music, Money & You
The Memoir

Managing the Business
Table of Contents

Foreword

I am honored to have the opportunity to share some of the things that I have learned in the entertainment business throughout the years. I have been a consultant to a select group of performers in the areas of vocal technique, style coaching, material selection, marketing, recording, and many other things. Several of my clients have asked me to write a book about my experiences, and my initial response was always, "Why would anyone want to hear about my experiences?" But it soon occurred to me that there are many performers that could benefit from someone else's life-long experience in the business. Performers often feel a great deal of frustration as they navigate their way around the obstacles encountered in the entertainment business. I would have loved having a mentor when I was starting out, and so, it is for those reasons that I have taken on the task of writing *Music, Money and You! Managing the Business.*

Introduction

Music, Money and You is a memoir of disappointment and triumph in the music business. Award-winning, internationally acclaimed vocalist, Greta Pope, has created a work to inspire, encourage, and challenge every performing artist to find their own greatness.

As a result of many of the technological advances of the 20th century, live music has suffered greatly. People often choose other entertainment options. In the early part of the 20th century, ordinary people could go out for a romantic night on the town and see Sarah Vaughn, Peggy Lee, Nat King Cole, Edith Piaf, Eartha Kitt, and many other great artists in wonderfully intimate venues across the country and around the world.

Over time, however, people began to choose other types of entertainment. Mega rock concerts, television, radio, audio recordings, movies, video games, and the like have all de-sensitized us to the human touch, the human voice, and human interaction. It is incumbent upon today's performing artist to create a superb product, build a fan base, and bring live music back to the beautiful venues of the world. As each artist cultivates a fan base for him or herself, that artist is cultivating an audience for all live music. Through many artists working together to renew the public interest in live music, there will be more and more opportunities for artists to work, and more opportunities for intimate live music to once again be a viable and preferred type of entertainment in the 21st Century.

In addition to being a memoir, *Music, Money and You* is also a how-to manual for managing the music business. Whether you're an artist, or someone planning to manage an artist, this book is for you. Dr. Greta Pope has prepared a simple, easy to read guide to put you on the right track to achieving your dreams.

Early Life

Music has been my life since childhood. I grew up in Cincinnati, Ohio at a time when life was simple and wonderful. My parents were educated, hardworking, loving, and patient. They had been married for fifteen years when I was born. My father was an engineer and my mother a housewife. Fourteen months after my birth, my brother Bill came along. Bill and I had an idyllic childhood. Our family lived in an old, Victorian brick home on Dayton Street in Cincinnati. It was a lovely home. My brother and I spent many wonderful hours playing in the fenced-in yard. We had a cute little cocker spaniel named Tubby. I have no idea how we settled on that name for the dog, but we adored Tubby.

My mother would play beautiful music for us on the piano. There was always music in our home. My parents had a vast collection of recordings ranging from classical instrumental music, to opera, to jazz, to popular music. They were quite knowledgeable about different styles of music and shared their knowledge with us. My mother and father sang often. Their duet repertoire included, "Indian Love Call," a beautiful love song from Rudolf Friml's operetta *Rose Marie*, originally sung by Nelson Eddy and Jeanette McDonald. This was my favorite. It was fantastic to hear their voices soaring, making such beautiful music together. Our family regularly attended the opera in Cincinnati, which at that time was a seasonal offering, held outdoors at the Cincinnati Zoo. We spent many great evenings at the "Zoo Opera" listening to world renowned operatic stars of the day. The opera performances were later housed at Cincinnati's Music Hall. The Cincinnati Opera is still going strong today. A little known fact about the Cincinnati Opera is that it is the second oldest opera company in the United States, having given its first performance in 1920. It is second only to the Metropolitan Opera in New York City.

On family road-trips, we would sing all kinds of songs. My parents sang in two-part harmony, encouraging my brother and me to sing the third part of the triad. This was not my brother's "thing," so he would sit quietly reading or playing a game while I listened, trying to insert the third part into their duet. I eventually became very good at picking out harmony parts.

I began playing piano at the age of five. We had a very beautiful piano at home that had belonged to my grandmother. My first teacher was Dorothy Ratterman. Mrs. Ratterman was the organist for our church and would come to my home each week for my piano lesson. She was a short, round, German woman with a very jovial smile. After a few years studying with her, Mrs. Ratterman suggested that my parents find me a teacher at the Cincinnati Conservatory of Music at the University of Cincinnati. Mrs. Ratterman felt that she had taken me as far as she could. I studied piano privately throughout the remaining years of my childhood at the Cincinnati Conservatory of Music. At the age of nine, I began taking violin lessons, primarily because my brother was playing violin. I loved the sound and look of the instrument. I also enjoyed the social aspect of playing in a string ensemble and orchestra. Practicing and playing piano can be very lonely. Though I never gave up the piano, I began studying the violin, and I came to love playing it.

While I was in high school, I played with the Woodward High School Orchestra, as well as in a string quartet. Each Sunday afternoon, my friends Debbie, George, and Mark would come over to my house to practice string quartet pieces. We spent hours playing together. My mother would prepare sandwiches and treats for us each week. We loved it! I played second violin in the quartet and my favorite piece was the Allegro Movement of Mozart's "Eine Kleine Nachtmusik." I became so enchanted with the violin that I auditioned and was accepted as a regular member of the first violin section of the Cincinnati Youth Symphony Orchestra. The Cincinnati Youth Symphony played under the baton of conductor Sigmund Effron, who was at that time the Concert Master of the world renowned Cincinnati Symphony Orchestra. Sigmund Effron also became my private violin teacher. I learned a great deal about music and hard work from him.

Sigmund Effron was a wonderful man with a great sense of humor. One of his favorite sayings that has stuck with me throughout my life was related to sight reading. When I played a wrong note, he would say, "The black is the note, the white is the paper." In other words, play what is written on the page! This sounds very simple, but it takes a great deal of practice to have the skill to always execute a phrase correctly. I learned to practice in a very focused way. I also learned that success in music and success in life is always the result of hard work.

As my high school career began to draw to a close, it was time to look toward the next stage of my life. The college search was truly an eye-opener. I looked at many colleges and universities before selecting the one that I would attend. My high school counselor, Mrs. Keys called me into her office one September day during my senior year in high school. Mrs. Keys was a wonderful counselor who took a tremendous interest in me. She sat me down for a chat and asked what my college plans were. I really didn't know. I knew that I would be going to college, but I had no idea where. I had been looking at schools, but at that point, I hadn't been terribly focused. I had good grades, I was a class officer, and I was involved in many school activities, including the drill team, orchestra, Ensemble (a very high caliber music organization), and a service group where I was an official greeter and ambassador for the school. I did not know it then, but that meeting would change my life.

The College Years

My guidance counselor, Mrs. Keys told me that she had submitted my name and information to a few colleges that she thought would be a good fit for me. They were all small private schools that would offer me special personal attention and guidance. Up to that point, I thought that I would go to the University of Cincinnati, as many of my friends were planning to attend. It was a superb university with tens of thousands of students, and I was very familiar with the campus. Plus, the Cincinnati Conservatory of Music was on the University of Cincinnati campus. I had been going there weekly for music lessons since I'd been a young girl.

My parents were very open to other college options, so we investigated the other schools suggested by Mrs. Keys. I had grown up in an extremely sheltered environment and my parents, particularly my father, were very concerned about selecting a safe college environment. We saw many very pretty campuses, but one in particular stood out. It was called The Western College for Women in Oxford, Ohio. Western was a beautiful 208 acre campus that had been founded in 1853 as The Western Female Seminary by Helen Peabody, a Mount Holyoke graduate. In 1894, it became The Western: A College and Seminary for Women under the Presidency of Leila McKee, a Wellesley graduate. This kind of legacy appealed to my parents, and the best part was that Western College was in Oxford, Ohio, only 35 miles from Cincinnati. Miami University was also in Oxford, so it was possible to have a social life involving men.

My dad thought that this was fantastic! I would live on campus, come home only on official holidays, but I would only be 35 miles away! My parents decided that The Western College for Women would be our choice. I have to say that I loved the school as well. It sat back off the road one full mile via a lovely winding drive. The buildings were old and elegant. Each discipline had its own superbly equipped center.

Western had a lovely dining hall where students enjoyed meals. Breakfast was served cafeteria style while lunch and dinner were served family style. It was important to arrive on time for meals. We stood behind our chairs and sang a lovely grace before being seated and served our meals. The tables were large and square. There were eight places per table (two on each side). We dined with faculty members at every meal and enjoyed very lively repartee.

Each dorm had a Housemother. She was the go-to person for any problems that the girls might have. She was a good source of information and a great listener. Each dorm also had a Parlor where the girls received gentlemen callers. Any girls who smoked cigarettes were allowed to smoke only in the Parlor. Walking on campus with a cigarette was strictly prohibited. Western was a short 20 minute walk from downtown Oxford. We often opted to walk, but the school also provided the Blue Western Van to drive us downtown and back for shopping or to go to the movies. The van made several trips per day.

The Western College for Women had a large population of international students. My freshman roommate, Claudette, was from Africa, specifically, the Ivory Coast (Cote d'Ivoire). Claudette had just arrived in America two days before classes began. What a culture shock for her − and me! However, we became fast friends and came to appreciate each other's cultures. Claudette went home with me to Cincinnati for school vacations. Spending time with her was a real treat for my family and friends. She was a great girl. I remember her excitement at the first snowfall. She began babbling in French and squealing at the top of her lungs. She had read about snow, but she'd never seen it in person. The entire dorm celebrated with her that day.

Having no idea of how cold it gets in Ohio, Claudette had purchased a jacket appropriate for a crisp autumn day in the Ohio Valley. She was not at all prepared for the damp chill and strong winds of a blustery Midwest winter. After all, Claudette was from a very hot climate. She didn't have a winter coat, hat, gloves, or boots. One chilly afternoon, we took a walk across campus to see Miss Brickman, the Foreign Student Advisor. Miss Brickman was good at solving all kinds of problems. She was able to arrange for the winter attire that Claudette needed. Claudette was from a wealthy family. Her parents were gold traders and they visited often during the time that Claudette was at The

Western College for Women.

I really enjoyed my interaction with Claudette and the other foreign students at Western. Many of the international students had already completed undergraduate degrees in their own countries. Girls from other countries were often sent to Western by their parents to improve their English skills and learn American culture. I was curious about the culture of these young women, and I longed for the international experiences that were available, so I joined the Miami University International Club.

During my sophomore year I had a large private room on a short corridor with only six rooms. There was an interesting mix of cultures living on that corridor and we had some of the most fascinating discussions about government, social issues, education, music, and art. We developed wonderful relationships and had great gatherings on the weekends. It was good wholesome fun.

Junior year, I had a roommate from Sweden, and senior year, a roommate from Japan. This was fantastic exposure for me. It opened my eyes and my mind in a very special way. Several of my roommates, and many of the friends that I had while at Western, are still my friends today. Each June, The Western College Alumnae Association has a reunion. Alumnae come from all over the world to see each other again. The Western College for Women was a unique experience and affected my life immensely. It set the stage for my life of international pursuits.

The Vocal Beginning

I began college not really knowing what I wanted to do. I knew that I'd have to go to graduate school, but I wasn't sure what type of career I wanted. I considered law; my dad wanted me to be a teacher; and a physician friend of my family was encouraging me to be a doctor. I personally did not have a clue! I went to college hoping that a discipline I could love would find me, and it did! I finished college in four years with a Bachelor of Liberal Arts Degree with an emphasis in Music. During my time at Western, I participated in many activities, including the all female Western College choir. There is no sound quite like the sound of a women's choir. The voices are so delicate and pure, like bells ringing. We learned many well known sacred and secular choral pieces written for women's voices. It was a wonderful experience. Through the Western choir, I became familiar with yet another type of music.

I was able to sight read music very well, and as a result, became the darling of the choir director. I had always enjoyed singing in the privacy of my own room, but I had never sung in a public forum. Now suddenly I was being asked to sing solos with the choir. This was quite surprising but very flattering and enjoyable to me. I found that my sense of pitch was good as a result of my years studying the violin. It was also very easy for me to learn new music because I played the piano. I began singing more and more. Within the first month, I was offered a scholarship to take private voice lessons at the college. I was delighted. My new voice teacher was Joan Gersten. Through my study with her, my vocal range began to widen and my voice rapidly developed into a legitimate musical instrument. I seemed to have a natural ability for singing and I felt as though my previous musical training had laid the groundwork for a career as a performer of vocal music.

My voice teacher was a member of the Richmond Opera Company in Richmond, Indiana. The Richmond Opera Company was planning several performances of *The Magic Flute*, a charming and very well known opera by Wolfgang Amadeus Mozart. My teacher was singing the dramatic coloratura role of the Queen of the Night. It was a magnificent and exciting role requiring a great deal of vocal skill and acting ability. I went with her to one of the rehearsals and was thrilled by everything that I saw and heard. It was absolutely fabulous! Though I was still quite inexperienced as a singer, after seeing my enthusiasm, my teacher suggested that I audition for a role that had not yet been filled in *The Magic Flute*. It was the role of Papagena, the bird girl. I couldn't believe that she was suggesting that I could be in the production. She contacted the Director, got me an audition, and I got the role! I was so excited. The Papagena character sang one piece in the opera. It was a duet with Papageno, the bird man. Though Papagena was a small role, it left an indelible impression upon me and I was never quite the same.

I had another wonderful experience in November of my freshman year. Though I had just begun to study voice, my teacher encouraged me to audition for the Metropolitan Opera Regional Auditions held at the University of Cincinnati. She felt that singing and auditioning anywhere and everywhere would help me to overcome stage fright and gain confidence. I agreed to audition. My only audition to date had been for the role of Papagena, and that audition had been in a small practice room and had involved only two people – the Director and me. I had no idea what a Metropolitan Opera audition would be like.

I arrived at the University about 30 minutes before the auditions began. I parked my car and began walking toward the building where the auditions were to be held. I found myself walking alongside a very beautiful, soft spoken, young African American woman. We began to chat and she asked me if I was auditioning. I told her yes and that I had only been studying for two months, but that my teacher wanted me to do as many auditions as possible so that I would get used to the process. She asked what I was singing and I told her that I'd be singing "O Mio Babbino Caro" from Puccini's 1918 opera *Gianni*

Schicchi. She said that she was familiar with that aria. I asked what she would be singing, and she told me the name of an aria that I had never heard of before. By this time, we had reached the auditorium where the auditions were to be held. We wished each other luck and went our separate ways inside the auditorium. I was sitting silently in the back of the auditorium, scared to death, wondering what I was doing there. I was seventeen years old, but I must have looked like I was twelve. I was horrified!

After listening to a few auditions, I left the auditorium to go to the ladies room to muster the necessary courage for my audition. I saw several of the other singers talking about how they might as well go home because "Kathy" was auditioning. I wondered who this Kathy was, and then went back into the auditorium, took my seat, and continued listening to the auditions.

The Metropolitan Opera Audition panel does not call singers by name when it's their turn to audition. They refer to them by an assigned number. This practice helps the panel to be objective. Often, the names of exceptionally talented singers get around amongst people in the operatic community. Therefore, in order to prevent the judges from being biased, singers are assigned a number.

My number was finally called. I walked to the stage, stated my number and the aria that I was singing. I could see the panel of judges smile. They could see that I was very young and inexperienced, but they were patient and extremely kind to me. When I finished singing my aria, they complimented me on my lovely voice, told me to continue to practice, and encouraged me to return to the auditions the following year. I was thrilled by the encouragement that they had given me. I thanked them and quickly returned to my seat. Soon after I sat down, the panel called another number and a hush fell over the audience. My new friend from the parking lot rose and made her way to the stage. I was anxious to hear her sing. She was so beautiful and she had been so nice to me. She stated her audition number and told the panel that she was singing Suzanna's very beautiful aria from Mozart's *Le Nozze di Figaro* (The Marriage of Figaro) entitled "Deh, Vieni, Non Tardar." The pianist began the introduction, and then, the most angelic voice I had ever heard began to caress the notes and the melody of the beautiful aria. There were trills and runs and soaring high notes. It was absolutely beyond anything that I could possibly have imagined. My new friend turned out to be the great Kathleen Battle. This was the "Kathy" that the women had been speaking of in the ladies room. Kathy Battle won the Regional Metropolitan Opera auditions that day, and she went on to win the National Metropolitan Opera Auditions.

Soon thereafter, she was the darling of the Metropolitan Opera stage, singing the great coloratura roles of the operatic repertoire. Several months after she won the Met Auditions, she came to Cincinnati to appear in a concert version of Gounod's *Faust* with the great bass Michael Devlin in the role of Mephistopheles. I was lucky enough to have been selected to be in the chorus for that production. Kathy Battle sang the role of Siebel, Faust's student, from the rear balcony. It was fantastic! Approximately one year later, Kathy came to Miami University in Oxford Ohio to perform a concert. I went to the concert and sat in the front row. I was mesmerized by her voice and presence. After the concert, she welcomed me backstage and autographed my program. She had come a long way since the day that I met her, but she was still the same sweet person that I called my friend. I still have that autographed program that Kathy gave me. It is one of the treasures of my life. It hangs beautifully framed in my kitchen where I can enjoy it every day.

About five years ago, I went to a Kathleen Battle concert at Symphony Center in Chicago. She looked fantastic and she sang beautifully. The audience demanded five encores that evening. Kathleen Battle is truly one of the greatest operatic divas of the late 20th and early 21st centuries. She is my friend.

Gospel, Opera and Amusement Parks

I continued to study operatic roles and I got many opportunities to perform those roles. I studied the history of opera, learning about the writing styles of different composers. I studied Italian, French, German, and Spanish so that I could sing easily in those languages. My teacher gave me wonderful direction and I continued to blossom musically. It was exciting and fulfilling.

While at Western, I met two classmates who were wonderful gospel singers. They were looking for a third singer to form a group with them. My family had been Episcopalian and I hadn't had any exposure to gospel music. I explained this to them, but they wanted me anyway. They needed a high voice. Western was a very small school of approximately 300 women, so they didn't have a lot of people to choose from. I agreed to sing with them, eager for this new cultural experience. I was particularly motivated because, as an African American, this was an opportunity to get closer to my own community in experiencing and participating in this fabulous style of music. Through these two talented girls, Phyllis Adkins and JoAnn McCorkle, I had an opportunity to gain greater appreciation for the richness of my own culture. We named our singing group The Gospel Motets and we became quite the rage in Oxford.

Western had a very beautiful facility called Kumler Chapel that had been designed after a chapel based in a small Normandy Village. Each Sunday morning, there was a chapel service where the choir performed regularly. The Gospel Motets also began doing weekly performances at Chapel. We sang very lovely traditional gospel songs in three part harmony, but we also sang the hand-clappin', toe-tappin', feel-good kind of gospel. People loved it. Word got around, and after a while, the Chapel was packed with Western and Miami students and faculty, as well as people from the community. All came to see the Gospel Motets. There would be standing room only.

Phyllis' father was the minister at the largest Pentecostal Church in Dayton, Ohio. We went to that church to sing, and suddenly, we had all kinds of offers to do weekend tours. We were "on the road" singing gospel! During my senior year, I had a proposal of marriage from a widowed minister with six children. Yikes!!! His oldest child was older than I was. I graciously declined his proposal. That was the end of my gospel career.

Also during my senior year, Mrs. Gersten told me of an opera that she was performing with the Dean of the School of Fine Arts at Miami University. This was a two character opera called *The Telephone* by Gian Carlo Menotti. *The Telephone* is an opera about a gentleman named Ben who is trying desperately to telephone a young woman named Lucy to ask her for a date, but he's unable to get through because she is always on the telephone gossiping with her girl friends. It's a very funny opera. At the end of it, Ben reaches Lucy and she says yes to the date. My teacher suggested that I understudy her role of Lucy. It is a very difficult coloratura role, but I figured what harm could there be in understudying this role. I'd never be called upon to perform it. Well, much to my surprise and horror, Mrs. Gersten very thoughtfully invited me to perform the role for one of the performances. This was to have been her performance opportunity. It was an extremely generous gesture as she was putting my interests ahead of her own by sharing the role with me. I was grateful, but I was also mortified. With the guidance of my voice teacher, I worked very hard to learn and memorize the role. The Dean and I had many rehearsals together and the performance date finally arrived. The performance went swimmingly. The local newspapers covered it, and my teacher was very proud of me. To this day, I appreciate Mrs. Gersten for the many wonderful opportunities that she gave me. As a result of my performance in *The Telephone*, I was offered a full scholarship to Miami University to study toward a Master of Music Degree in Vocal Performance. I decided to attend graduate school at Miami University, and within one full calendar year, I had completed all of the requirements and received the Master of Music Degree.

During the summers of my college years, I gained experience performing other styles of music. Andrea, one of my girlfriends, suggested that we both audition for summer amusement park work. We spent many hours practicing together. I would play piano for her vocal audition and then she would play piano for mine. This was going to be fun. We weren't going to be singing our usual classical music. Instead, we'd be singing music from the Broadway stage. How exciting!

We each had to prepare two songs, one ballad and one up-tempo. We went to the Miami University music library and combed through the many Broadway scores, finally settling on the songs that we wanted to sing. The date of the audition arrived and we traveled by car to Cincinnati where the auditions were being held. We signed in and submitted our photos and resumes. We were then directed to a very long line of people waiting to audition. There were about 30 available performer slots for the amusement park shows, but there were hundreds, perhaps thousands of people auditioning. It was unbelievable! We waited and waited and waited. Finally, after several hours, we reached the front of the line. We were up! We went into the audition room together. First Andrea sang her prepared songs and I played piano. When she finished, the panel of judges announced that she would be called back for the dance audition. This was great! Andrea and I then switched positions and I was on the hot-seat. I sang my prepared songs while Andrea played for me. The judges also called me back for the dance audition. Bingo! We were both very excited. We thanked the judges and floated out of the audition room. We were told where to go for the dance audition. We had worn our dance clothing under our street clothing in the hope of being invited to the dance audition. We went to the ladies room, organized ourselves, and ran to the dance audition.

The dance audition was challenging. It consisted of being shown 32 measures (or in dancer terms "four counts of eight") of a choreographed dance routine. After two or three trial runs, we were expected to do the choreography with style, smiles, and personality. As a young girl, I had studied ballet, tap, and modern dance at the Cincinnati Conservatory of Music. Part of my dance training had been developing the ability to learn dance steps quickly. Years of dance training turned out to be extremely beneficial in this case, as the amusement park shows required extensive singing and dancing skills.

This experience turned out to be one of the first difficult situations of my young career. Several days later, I received a call telling me that I had been hired as a singer/dancer for the Live Shows department at Cedar Point Amusement Park. Unfortunately, my friend Andrea did not get the job because her dance skills were not strong enough. I felt terrible about this turn of events and contemplated not taking the job. I was very happy to have gotten an opportunity to perform at Cedar Point, but I felt awful that my friend had not also been selected for the shows. After all, it had been her idea to audition!

Being the good friend that she was, Andrea encouraged me to take the job. She was genuinely happy for me, though I know she was disappointed not to have been hired as well. I learned through that experience that talented people don't always get the gig. Andrea was a very talented singer and actor, and she was a very beautiful girl, but this particular job required something that she just didn't have − the ability to learn dance steps easily and quickly.

Each performer has skills and talents that are unique to them. Andrea seemed to understand this. She went on to audition for summer-stock theater, and she was hired to do a series of musicals with the summer stock company. Her skills were more suited for that type of work. She loved it and they loved her. I was thrilled to know that Andrea had found something that she loved and for which she was perfectly suited. She was tenacious in her pursuit of finding performance work, and she found success.

This was a huge lesson for me. Things don't always work out the first time. It's important that we assess our strengths and seek things that are commensurate with those strengths. It's also important that we always work to improve our skills and increase our strengths. Andrea enrolled in dance classes right away. She worked hard at it and eventually became a very good dancer. The people that find success in life are the ones that have a clear understanding of their strengths and strive to improve their weaknesses. They are the ones that seek the right opportunities and that don't give up. Andrea had a good understanding of these concepts early in life. She worked summer stock throughout her college career, and upon graduation, she went on to have a professional career in musical theater and has spent her life performing on Broadway and in Broadway touring companies.

While Andrea went to work for summer stock, I went to Cedar Point

Amusement Park and had a great time performing at Cedar Point's *Golden Palace Theater.* We were a cast of four performers, singing and dancing scenes from early 20th century operetta. I was a coloratura soprano. One of the pieces that I performed was the very flamboyant, coloratura piece entitled "The Italian Street Song" from Victor Herbert's *Naughty Marietta.* I loved this style of singing. It was similar to singing the operatic repertoire, but it was more like musical theater. There was a wonderful tenor in the cast that sang "Rosabella" from Frank Loesser's musical *Most Happy Fella.* I also sang "Someday I'll Find You," a beautiful song by Noel Coward. I loved this music! It was an opportunity to sing in the *bel canto* or beautiful singing style. It was a great summer of beautiful music, new friends, and fantastic fun!

The next summer I worked at King's Island Amusement Park. Performing in the live shows department at both of these amusement parks was a fun and lucrative way to spend the summers. Well, lucrative for a college student. We would sing and dance five performances per day. It was tedious at times, but I learned to muster enthusiasm even when I wasn't feeling it. My motto was, "The audience that sees the fifth show of the day has paid the same entry fee as the audience that saw the first show of the day." Every audience deserves a great performance, no matter how tired the performers may be. I challenged myself to perform with a high level of energy and enthusiasm every time. Through these shows I learned to "dig deep." This was a great lesson that I continue to apply to all areas of my life.

Ethnomusicologist or Tap Dancer?

After receiving my Master's Degree, I went to Indiana University in Bloomington, Indiana and studied for a Doctor of Philosophy Degree in ethnomusicology. Ethnomusicology is the study of music in culture. I arrived at IU and registered for my classes. I was required to take many advanced music history and music theory classes, as well as many classes in anthropology.

While studying ethnomusicology at Indiana, I was very fortunate to have been selected to study voice with the great Eileen Farrell. This was actually quite unusual because I was not seeking a degree in vocal performance. Eileen Farrell was a very famous singer and a highly coveted vocal instructor. She had sung roles with the Metropolitan Opera in New York City, The Lyric Opera in Chicago, The San Francisco Opera, and other well known opera companies in America and abroad. It was an honor and a privilege to work with her. She taught me many wonderful things about singing and about being a stage performer. Though Miss Farrell was a famed opera singer, she also dabbled in performing show tunes and other popular styles of music, making her very much a "Renaissance Woman." I had already begun my own journey with regard to singing different styles of music, in addition to studying and performing the operatic repertoire. Ms. Farrell was very supportive and encouraging of this.

I enjoyed my studies at Indiana University. The IU Music School is one of the best in the world and the caliber of faculty and students is top notch. During my second year in the doctoral program, I received a call to perform for a television commercial for King's Dominion Amusement Park in Richmond, Virginia. King's Dominion was, at that time, a sister park to King's Island. This commercial was going to be filmed in Richmond, Virginia, and I would be tap dancing with Dick Van Dyke. This was absolutely thrilling! Dick Van Dyke is a famous actor and dancer, whose career spanned six decades. He is best known for his roles in the films *Bye Bye Birdie, Mary Poppins,* and *Chitty Chitty Bang Bang*, as well as the television series, *The Dick Van Dyke Show* and

Diagnosis Murder. He is an American icon! I asked my professors if I could be excused from class for one week to go to Virginia and do the commercial. I asked for assignments in advance so that I could keep up with my class work. I felt that this was a great opportunity and was stunned when my Anthropology professor replied to my request with, "Do you want to be an ethnomusicologist or a tap dancer?" I couldn't believe it! He was making me choose between two passions – studying music in culture and having a practical experience in show business! It seemed to me that having an opportunity for practical application of the performance skills that I had learned would have been a terrific thing. My professor had a different idea.

As it turns out, I did go to Richmond to do the commercial with Dick Van Dyke. It was great fun and a real learning experience. Soon thereafter, I made the decision to enjoy the opportunities that I was getting to travel and work in the "business of show." I decided to put my Ph.D. on hold and pursue a performing career with the intention of eventually going back to school to complete my degree.

Upon hearing of my thoughts about leaving school, my parents were not happy. Though they had encouraged me to study music during my formative years, they were not in favor of a performance career. From everything that they had seen and heard, a performance career was very difficult and unpredictable. In their opinion, it was fraught with dangers and would not offer me a solid, secure and happy life. My dad and mother wanted me to complete the Ph.D. and become a professor at a major university. My dad felt that once I got a faculty position at a university, I might meet a gallant gentleman in academia, get married, and have a family. He felt that I needed someone to take care of me.

It turned out that within two months of my decision to leave Indiana University, my father became very ill and subsequently passed away in September. My heart was broken. My father had been my teacher, my friend, and my confidant. He was a very wise man and I was his princess. I was a very lucky girl to have had such a gentle and loving father. Daddy was encouraging me to get settled because he might have sensed that he would not be around to look after me. One of the last things that I remember him saying to me was, "Find a nice young man, get married, and be happy."

I would soon meet the man of my dreams.

Leaving Academia

The November after my father's death, my mother and I decided to take a trip and spend some time in New York City. We had friends there. We spent time sight-seeing, shopping, and enjoying wonderful shows on Broadway. The trip was very therapeutic for my mother and for me. We had an opportunity to grieve, bond, and share our feelings. My mother assured me that she would be supportive of whatever career choice I made. This gave me the confidence to leave the doctoral program at Indiana University and pursue my dreams.

Once I left academia, I was offered a full-time job as a musical director with King's Productions Company, which was the company that owned and produced all of the shows for King's Island Amusement Park in Mason, Ohio; King's Dominion Amusement Park in Richmond, Virginia; Carowinds Amusement Park in Charlotte, North Carolina; Great America Amusement Park in Santa Clara, California; Canada's Wonderland Amusement Park in Toronto Ontario, Canada; and Australia's Wonderland in Sydney, New South Wales, Australia. I worked as a musical director for several years, writing musical arrangements, auditioning and selecting performers to participate in the shows, and serving as musical director during the rehearsal phase of the shows. It was a wonderful job and a wonderful opportunity to travel and build a career with the company.

In an attempt to prepare me for a managerial position, I was given a position in the Operations/Management side of the business. This was very interesting to me. I learned a lot about the day-to-day managing of the entertainers, musicians, choreographers, musical arrangers and directors, and costume designers. I also learned a great deal about the process of set building, sound, lighting, and all of the technical aspects of mounting a big production. I oversaw facility maintenance, and I learned to manage people. This was a wonderful experience as it gave me a new perspective on show business. The public, when watching a show, only sees the performer. They generally have no idea of all of the people involved behind the scenes of every production. The performers are important, true enough, but there are many, many people without whom the performers would be lack-luster. The creative people behind the scenes create the magic and mystique of show business. The sound and lighting designers, the costume designers, the set designers, and all of the crew that bring those wonderful designs to life are an integral part of the overall production. The work that these people do is to be respected and celebrated. They pour their hearts and souls into their work. Performers should always be mindful that set designers, costume designers, or lighting designers invest the same energy and commitment into their job as the performer puts into theirs. Everyone's work should be respected and appreciated.

I worked for a year in this position, and though I enjoyed it and appreciated the opportunity that the company was giving me, I missed performing. I expressed my feelings to the company management. Fortunately, they had been very happy with the job that I was doing and they suggested that I serve as performer/company manager for shows that they were sending abroad. This was perfect! I was able to perform while continuing to develop my management skills in yet another arena.

I agreed to perform and manage a U.S.O. Tour that was headed for a three month engagement in the Far East. I was the featured performer in a show that consisted of a band of five musicians – two female backup singers, a roadie (a man that sets up stage equipment), and a sound and lighting man. Off we went on a wonderful adventure!

We flew from Cincinnati, Ohio to Travis Air Force Base in Fairfield, California and then on to Elmendorf Air Force Base in Anchorage, Alaska. We arrived in Anchorage at 2:00 in the afternoon. It was extremely cold and it was very dark! What a shock! I had heard that Alaska was dark for extended periods of time in the winter, but I couldn't believe what I was seeing. It was incredible! Our assigned officer met us, took us for a meal, and then got us settled in. We performed our show that evening for the troops. We had been in rehearsals for the show for several weeks prior, and we had performed the show for family, friends and company management. However, this was our first experience performing for the G.I.s, and we were very pleasantly surprised by how much they enjoyed and appreciated our performance. They cheered, clapped their hands, and stomped their feet. They wanted to meet us after the show and we were delighted to receive them. It was very rewarding to perform for the guys and gals that keep America safe. We knew that through this U.S.O. Tour, we were in for a really unique experience.

The next morning, we headed to Japan. From that point on, we were given military officer status which allowed us to have many of the privileges that officers had. We were officially part of the American armed forces and we were proud to be bringing American culture and music to our service people overseas. We made the trip to Japan on the Flying Tiger Airline which carried cargo and soldiers. There were not many amenities for our comfort. I remember receiving our first meal on the plane. Each passenger was given a box containing food. As a matter of fact, the boxes were tossed to us. There were three sandwiches, three small cartons of milk, fruit, cookies, and several other items of food in each box. I remember thinking that these guys must be really hungry! It seemed that there was enough food in one box to feed our entire band! During that flight, we were served three meals. We spent our time eating, sleeping, and getting to know the soldiers who were being dispatched to the military bases in Japan. They were delightful.

After a very long flight, we landed in Japan. We had a 48 hour opportunity to recover from traveling, and then we began a very rigorous travel and performance schedule. We performed at all of the military installations. It was great. As company manager, I found that there were many things to manage, including making sure that all of the equipment arrived on time at every destination. Managing the band and tech guys was no easy feat. We often had to leave our hotel early in the morning in order to arrive at our show venue on time. Frequently, we had to be flown by helicopter to remote performance locations, so it was crucial that everyone got up and met our ground transportation provider on time. We had several close calls, but we always made it.

On days off, I often sought lone activities so that I wouldn't have to be responsible for anyone else. Everyone was on their own. One day, I ventured into Tokyo to see if I could find the Saks Fifth Avenue department store which was advertised in all the fashion magazines. I thought that it would be easy, and that I could enjoy a little shopping on my day off. The Tokyo subway lines are color coded. How hard could this be? I took the yellow line from the military base so all I had to do was take the yellow line back – except it wasn't that simple. I found the Ginza (shopping area) and browsed through some of the stores. Of course I couldn't talk to anyone or ask any questions as I didn't speak a word of Japanese. People were staring at me because I looked different, but there was no hostility in their faces. During this time, there were no women soldiers fighting in the military, so there weren't many American women in Tokyo, and there certainly weren't many African American women there. I was a novelty and the people were very curious about me. They stopped in their tracks and gaped. I smiled at them and they smiled back. One woman with her young daughter came up to me and caressed my face. It was very sweet. We couldn't communicate in language, but we communicated with our eyes.

After an hour or so, I decided to head back to the base. Suddenly, I was completely turned around and confused. I don't know what happened, but I couldn't remember which way I needed to go to get back to the subway. I told myself not to panic and to try and ask someone. I figured someone spoke English. Unfortunately, I wasn't able to find anyone who spoke English, but then, off in the distance, I saw a small uniformed man standing outside what looked like a phone booth. I immediately rushed over to him and began asking him where the subway was. He just stood looking at me with a smile on his face. After a few minutes, there were ten small uniformed men standing around me. They were policemen and they were there to help! The only problem was that they couldn't understand me and I couldn't understand them!

It was all very friendly, and after a while, we all began laughing. Finally, one of them went into the little structure that looked like a phone booth. It was a Police Box with a phone inside. This gentleman dialed a number, said a few words in Japanese and handed the phone to me. There was an English speaking voice on the other end of the line. I was so relieved, and so were the policemen. The policeman that called had told the voice where I was. All I had to do was to tell him that I was looking for the yellow subway line and that I was an

American U.S.O. entertainer headed back to the military base. He told me to wait right there, and that he would send a car to take me back. Within five minutes, a small police car pulled up and the driver gestured to me to get in. I did, and he gave me first class service back to the base. He spoke English very well, and along the ride back to the base, he pointed out several landmarks and told me interesting facts about Tokyo. All is well that ends well, but I never ventured out alone again.

Thirty-One Pieces

During the course of the tour, I was constantly counting people and pieces of equipment to make sure that everyone and everything was accounted for. We had eight performers, one roadie, one sound man, and 31 pieces of equipment, including sound, lighting, costumes, shoes, sheet music, instruments, and microphones, in addition to our personal luggage. Accounting for everyone and everything was daunting, at best.

I also did the advance work. It was my job to call ahead and make sure that everything would be ready when we arrived at the next location. We performed at all of the military bases in Japan, Korea, Hong Kong, the Philippines, Midway, and Hawaii. While in Japan, we visited Hiroshima, where we saw the devastation from the bombing of World War II. We also went to the Demilitarized Zone in Korea. Our assigned officer took us on a tour of the DMZ where we saw the dividing line between North and South Korea, with North Korean soldiers guarding their side of the border. We were close enough to touch them, but we were forbidden to touch them, speak to them, or even make eye contact with them, as we were warned that we might create a problem that could cause an international incident. Even though there was no war going on at the time, there was a great deal of tension in that region.

When we returned from our successful tour of the Far East, we were dispatched to a similar type of tour through Europe. We did our show at military installations across Germany, France, Italy, and Spain. We had an opportunity to talk to people in France that remembered the day that the American troops stormed the beaches of Normandy. They thanked us and told us how grateful they were to America. This was very moving. We heard wonderful stories at every destination that gave us a connection to the past and a real sense of America's impact on the world. Having visited these historic places as a representative of the United States of America is an experience that I shall never forget.

When I returned from my 15 month stint as a G.I. (Government Inspected) entertainer, I got a job as a featured singer and dancer in a Las Vegas-style show aboard the Norwegian Cruise Line ships. Again, I was company manger as the ensemble traveled each week between the Windward, Starward, Sunward, and Southward ships performing the Sea Legs Revue.

After fulfilling my six month contract on the small ships, I opted to accept another six month contract, this time aboard the S.S. Norway. The Norway, during those years, was the largest passenger cruise ship afloat. It had formerly been the S.S. France and had carried American and European aristocracy on transatlantic voyages. In 1962, the S.S. France had even transported Da Vinci's *Mona Lisa* from La Havre, France to New York City, as the legendary painting embarked upon an American tour. This was a very famous, historic vessel, and I was thrilled to have been selected to travel and perform in such a glamorous setting.

While working aboard the Norway, I had an opportunity to see many famous entertainers, including Carol Channing, Phyllis Diller, Dick Van Dyke, Sammy Davis Jr., Diahann Carroll, Martin Mull, Frank Sinatra, and Nipsy Russell, along with many others. I learned a lot by having the chance to see them perform their shows multiple times. I would watch the first show, then the second, then the third. During the first viewing, I was able to enjoy the show strictly for the entertainment value. In subsequent viewings, I would begin to watch for specific things, such as song choice and placement, show pacing, staging, lighting, sound techniques, and audience reaction. I would then watch for the overall affect that the show had on me and on other members of the audience.

These famous performers were always very kind to me. I was able to chat with them before and after shows. I had a million questions for the performers and for their crew. I received wonderful answers and insight into the business from everyone. Having the opportunity to study such high-level professionals, as well as their support crew, was huge for me. I watched their musicians, their security detail, their road managers, and their technicians. I had a chance to see how they interacted with the passengers when they weren't onstage. I knew that this was what I wanted to do. I wanted to tour my solo act in large venues with my own band.

The Love of My Life

While I was working as an entertainer onboard the S.S. Norway, I met the love of my life, my husband, Edward Wimp. He was a passenger with a convention of McDonald's owners from Chicago. A group of them came to the show on the Tuesday evening of the cruise. It was quite common for major American corporations to hold their annual conventions aboard the Norway as it was the largest, most luxurious cruise ship afloat. The one week cruises set sail from Miami, Florida and went from Sunday to Sunday. The ports on the itinerary were Curacao, Aruba, and a private island owned by NCL. On Wednesdays, the Norway dropped anchor for a day ashore in beautiful St. Thomas, U.S. Virgin Islands. All of the other cruise ships were able to pull up to the dock, but because of the Norway's size, the ship dropped anchor a mile or so out. Passengers had to go ashore on a tender, which was a small boat accommodating approximately 100 passengers at a time. Two tenders were deployed at once. One traveled from the Norway to St. Thomas while the other traveled from St. Thomas back to the Norway. The two tenders alternated routes for the entire time that the Norway was in port, providing transportation for the ship's passengers and crew.

It happened that my mother was traveling with me aboard the Norway the same week in January that Ed and the McDonald's folks were sailing. Mommy and I boarded the tender on that Wednesday morning and headed to St. Thomas. We did a little sight-seeing, a little shopping, had lunch, and boarded one of the late afternoon tenders back to the Norway. As we took our seats on the tender, a couple of the McDonald owners came over and complimented me on my performance in Tuesday evening's Sea Legs Revue. They then told me that there was a member of their party that wanted to meet me. They proceeded to introduce me to a very handsome gentleman by the name of Ed. Ed, my mother and I chatted on the trip back to the ship and when the tender reached the Norway, we went our separate ways.

That afternoon, my mother was scheduled for a massage. Before going to her massage, we went up to the pool deck for a little sun. Well, who did we see there? Why, Ed of course! He told us that his parents were also sailing that week and he invited us to join them at their table in the dining room. We accepted his invitation. Little did we know that this encounter was "kismet." Ed's parents were Edward and Kay (Kathryn) Wimp and they were delightful! We all immediately became friends. We spent many wonderful hours together during that week aboard the Norway. When the cruise ended on Sunday, Ed and his parents headed back to Chicago, my mother headed back to Cincinnati, and I remained on the Norway to "sing and dance my way into the hearts of millions!"

On that Sunday evening, I was called to the bridge of the ship to receive a phone call, which at that time was the only way to receive shore-to-ship calls. The bridge of the ship is command central, the pulse of the vessel. On that evening, one of the ship's officers made an announcement notifying me that I had a phone call and asking me to report immediately to the bridge. When I received this very public notification, I immediately became concerned that perhaps my mother was having difficulty getting home. I ran up to the bridge, answered the phone, and found that Ed was the caller. Not only was he calling to tell me that he and his parents had gotten home safely, but he had also called my mother to make sure that she had gotten home safely. This was a lovely gesture.

Edward Wimp was the owner of several McDonald's restaurants on the South Side of Chicago. He had made history when his corporation became the first African American organization to own a McDonald's restaurants in the history of the world. Ed had been the founding president of the Black McDonald's Owner-Operator Association (BMOA), which has now gone on to become a powerful national organization. Ed was a pioneer and a leader in American business. He was also a philanthropist and served on many not-for-profit boards around the city of Chicago. He was a great guy.

For the next week or so, Ed called me every day, and he did this until he received his phone bill. It was astronomical! Then he began writing me letters. Every single day! Our mail was delivered once a week on Sundays when we were in port in Miami, Florida. The ship's mail delivery man would tie Ed's seven letters together with a colorful ribbon and deliver them to me with much pomp and circumstance. Living aboard a ship is very much like living in a small town. Everyone knows everything about everybody. Well, as you can imagine, the entire ship (including the Captain) knew about Ed.

My S.S. Norway performance contract expired at the end of May. When my contract ended, Ed invited me to visit him in Chicago for a few days before heading back to Cincinnati. I was quite conservative and was therefore reluctant to visit him. I didn't know him well and, though I liked him, I just didn't know if a visit was the right thing to do at that time. I called my mother and asked if she remembered the guy that we had met aboard the Norway. I told her that he had invited me to visit him in Chicago. I was stunned when my mother asked me if I liked him. I couldn't believe that she was asking me this question, or that she would even consider encouraging me to visit a man that lived in another city. As it turned out, Ed had gotten my mother's blessing before asking me to visit. He had assured her that he was a gentleman, and he had asked her for my hand in marriage. I did go to visit him in Chicago, where he asked me to be his wife. I accepted, and the rest is history. We had a very small wedding at his parents' penthouse condominium in the Hyde Park neighborhood of Chicago. Judge Mark Jones of Chicago officiated, and on July 4th, we became husband and wife.

I wanted to continue performing after we married and Ed was in favor of this, so I began building my own one-woman show. There was a great deal of work involved with this. First, I had to select material that I liked and that was suitable for my voice and personal style. Then I wrote the arrangements, which involved determining the key and how the songs would begin and end. Deciding if there would be modulations (key changes) or if there would be any medleys (two or more songs joined together) was all part of the process. Once the arrangements were complete, I had an orchestrator write individual parts for 10 separate instruments. The show turned out very well. Utilizing these charts, I was able to easily work with any group of quality musicians. I often found myself in the position of entertainer, conductor, and musical director. When on the road, I would walk into a venue, meet a new group of musicians who were to be my band, rehearse with them, and do my show with them later that evening. It was quite challenging. During the show, I would conduct with my hands and sometimes by moving my entire body to establish the tempo. Eventually, I began traveling with a pianist conductor. By doing this, he could rehearse the pick-up band and conduct them during the show, allowing me to relax a little and come in for a brief sound check before the performance.

Before long, I began to get bookings for major corporate conventions. I did a show for an international convention of 10,000 McDonald's owners in Orlando, Florida. It was thrilling. I received a standing ovation! I also got bookings for my one-woman show on major cruise lines, including Norwegian, Royal Caribbean, Princess, and Holland America. I even performed my one-woman show for Pat Sajak and Vanna White on the "Wheel of Fortune" Cruise aboard the S.S. Norway. It was wonderful meeting and performing for them. I have developed several additional shows since that time. My one-woman shows continue to be in-demand for all types of events.

Now, I manage my own career as the result of a bad experience with a manager with whom I signed a one-year contract. Very soon after signing with him, I realized that I had made a mistake. Though he was a nice guy, he really did not have the contacts or the knowledge to help me, but it was too late. I was stuck in a one-year legally binding business relationship. I spent a year of my life not moving forward at all with my career. I didn't want this manager to file a lawsuit for breach of contract, so I adhered to the terms of the contract, which meant that I was not able to get work through any sources that didn't involve him. Yet I had many contacts of my own that he wanted me to share with him. I refused to do this as these were *my* contacts and I had worked hard to cultivate these relationships. I needed this manager to bring new opportunities to the table, but he was only interested in the contacts and relationships that I already had. I found that he'd never had any success in the entertainment business, and that he didn't know what he was doing.

This experience changed me immensely. I realized that it's important to really do your research before becoming involved with someone who is offering management service. Being a manager is not an easy job. This experience was the catalyst for beginning my studies toward a Doctorate Degree in Business Administration. I wanted to know more about entertainment management, not only for the sake of my career, but also to be able to help other performers understand the business and not be taken advantage of by people promising them things that they can't deliver. Ever since I had left the Indiana University doctoral program, I had wanted to go back and earn my Ph.D, and this seemed like the perfect time. I would work toward a Ph.D. and complete my Doctoral Dissertation on the topic of Entertainment Management. It took me five years, but I completed the coursework and dissertation and I now hold a Ph.D. in Business Administration.

Last year, an attorney was in one of my audiences. He saw the show, enjoyed it, and approached me about being my manager. I asked what kind of law he practiced and if he'd ever had any experience in the entertainment field. He told me that he was a criminal attorney and that he had never had any experience with entertainers. I was, and continue to be, reluctant to become involved with him. Though I am sure that he is knowledgeable about the law, entertainment law is a beast of its own and involves a lot of contacts in the entertainment business. I don't want to have to show someone how to manage my career. I want a manager that understands every aspect of the business and can lead *me* in a positive direction.

I know a lot about managing the career of a performing artist because I have been managing my own career for many years. I have seen the things that work and the things that don't. I am not opposed to taking on a manager. As a matter of fact, I would like to have someone working on my behalf, but that person would need to have great contacts, be very hard working, and be aggressive. They would also have to have experience in the entertainment field. Having a manager would allow me more time to spend on performing, learning new music, writing arrangements, consulting with performer clients, and doing book tours and such. If an artist is working regularly, it's very nice to have someone else to handle the details of a busy career, but be sure that the manager that you select can offer you the qualities that you need to move your career forward. Do your research first!

Finding the Right Niche

Throughout the 20th century, performers have sought the guidance of managers. There has always been a need for the entertainment "broker" to cultivate the talent and connect the talent with all of the people necessary to secure work, manage money, and provide legal advice. Recently, the Internet has provided new opportunities for building relationships and seeking work. In this modern era, we have the benefit of social networking sites, as well as the ability to browse the Web and send an email to just about anyone that we'd like. Although these new modes of communication are wonderful, they require persistence and a great deal of time in order to be effective. It is hard for performers to stay on top of their craft, learn new music, practice, perform, and still have the time to manage all of the other aspects of their career. There is still today, perhaps more than ever before, a need for the entertainment manager.

Through my years of experience in the business, I have seen that it is not easy for talented, trained entertainers to get good management. I have observed a dearth of knowledgeable, experienced managers in the industry. There are not many individuals or companies offering direction and support for the talented, ambitious artist. This is particularly true for the artist just starting out. Once an artist has a developed track-record, he or she can often secure representation with one of the major management companies, but for the unknown artist, it's very difficult to find good, knowledgeable, and trustworthy representation. The major management companies are very capable and successful at providing top-notch guidance to their artists, making them stand-outs in the entertainment field. Lesser known artists are frequently unable to find reliable, knowledgeable guidance to move their careers forward.

There are many career tracks for entertainers wanting to make a living in the business. Of course, it is safe to say that every entertainer dreams of becoming a huge star with world-wide recognition, great wealth, and the many privileges that go along with those things. However, the reality is that most performers will never reach that level of success. Entertainment is an extremely competitive business. For every act that makes it big, there are tens of thousands of acts, many of them perhaps just as talented, that will never make it at all. Most of them give up the dream and spend their lives working in totally unrelated fields, only occasionally dreaming of what might have been.

There is opportunity in the entertainment industry for second, third, fourth, and even fifth tier entertainers. These entertainers need guidance in understanding their available options. Often in colleges, music conservatories and dance studios, students are trained for very traditional career tracks. These include orchestras, opera companies, jazz bands, rock bands, and professional dance companies. With the right guidance, support and encouragement, these artists can apply their highly developed talents and skills to other viable performance arenas.

While this book will be very helpful in opening the eyes of the would-be artist to open-minded thinking regarding their career, it is also geared for the business professional with an interest in providing solutions to performers wanting to build a career in the entertainment industry. It will give the business professional insight into the industry, aiding them in developing the skills necessary to work with an established large management company, or to develop their own stable of performers and create a successful, independent management company of their own.

There are many areas of performing that an artist can aspire to today, including becoming a major performing artist or a back-up performer for a major artist. An artist can also choose to perform in Las Vegas style revue shows; children's shows and recordings; religious shows and recordings; studio work; college tours; festivals; cruise ships; amusement parks; voice-overs; TV commercials; and film, just to mention a few. Artists need knowledgeable guidance in selecting an area of entertainment suitable for their talent and ambition, as well as a strategy for attaining success in their chosen area. This book is designed to prepare the performer to be the driving force in creating, supporting and sustaining a successful career in the entertainment business.

Sincerity is Key

Today, I am performing my one-woman shows with The Greta Pope Orchestra. We entertain in many types of venues, performing for different types of audiences, including corporate audiences, festival audiences, jazz club audiences, cabaret audiences, cruise ship audiences, university audiences, children's audiences, family audiences, senior audiences, Christian audiences, Jewish audiences, and international audiences. We have performed on major cruise lines, at major world festivals, at leading cabaret rooms across America, at major corporate events across the country, and at wonderful concert venues worldwide. The Greta Pope Orchestra consists of a ten piece group, including Greta Pope with nine musicians, including piano, bass, drums, guitar, trumpet, saxophone, trombone, two background vocals, and Greta Pope. In addition to the orchestra, I work with my jazz duo, trio or quartette. I often perform my cabaret shows with only one musician – a pianist or a guitarist.

I am President and CEO of Greta Pope Entertainment, Inc., (GPE, Inc.) an Illinois corporation that produces live performances, radio shows and recording projects. GPE, Inc. provides and promotes quality entertainment worldwide. We are an entertainment production and publishing company. We produce multi-disciplinary, arts-in-education programming, as well as The American Vocal Workshop, which is a series of workshops designed to teach adults and children proper vocal technique for singing and speaking. I present vocal master classes, as well as entertainment management seminars. I also serve as a consultant to individual performers, as well as to the Chicago Public Schools.

I have had many wonderful opportunities to work with famous entertainers. This has given me a chance to ask them questions and to watch them perform front and center. The most significant thing that I have learned from these high profile performers is how to communicate with an audience. There are many things, aside from the actual performance, that are crucial to success on the stage. I emphasize these things with my clients and in my performances. Building a sincere relationship with the audience is a very important aspect of a good performance. Audiences like to feel as though they know the performer, and good entertainers make the audience feel very comfortable, as if they are in the entertainer's living room. There is an intimacy that occurs, even in the largest of venues. The audience wants to like the performer and feel as though they have a personal relationship with the performer. Sincerity is key. Most importantly, an entertainer must understand that a good performance is not about the performer, it's about the audience. It's about the performer connecting with each individual audience member and giving them something meaningful. As performers, we have the ability to connect with others in an unparalleled way. Through careful crafting of our presentations, we can evoke tears, laughter, and many other emotions. The performer's relationship with his or her audience is very special indeed.

Kay

I am very honored and privileged to be the daughter-in-law of American vocalist, Kay Davis. After graduating from Northwestern University with a Bachelor of Music Degree in 1942 and a Master of Music Degree in 1943, Kay Davis was sought out by the great Duke Ellington to be a member of his renowned orchestra.

Kay tells the story of preparing for her graduate recital with great enthusiasm. She had spent an entire college career learning and perfecting the material that she would perform on this very special occasion. All of her friends and family were on hand for this lifetime event. As the lights dimmed, a hush fell over the audience. The beautiful Kay Davis walked onto the stage with her pianist. She took her place in the bow of the piano and sang an exquisite program. After she sang her last note, the audience was on their feet applauding. Suddenly, the rear door of the recital hall opened, and there stood the great Duke Ellington. The audience immediately recognized him, and what should have been Kay's shining moment turned into a Duke Ellington autograph frenzy. Initially, she was disappointed, but it quickly became clear that the Duke had come specifically to see her performance. He had been listening from outside the door and was quite impressed by her. That evening, Duke Ellington offered Kay a position in his orchestra, and three days later, she went on the road with the band.

Kay Davis traveled the world with the Duke Ellington Orchestra from 1944 to 1950. In those days, Blacks were not able to stay at the major hotels, but instead, had to stay at Black owned hotels and private homes in the various cities that they traveled to. Information on available lodging for Blacks was readily available through the entertainer pipeline in those days. *The Chicago*

Defender and other African American publications frequently advertised these special overnight facilities. These inns were owned by Blacks, and they offered comfortable accommodations not only to entertainers, but to Blacks traveling under all circumstances. The accommodations were very nice, offering great home-cooked food and a social outlet for travelers.

Kay has also told me stories of the band having to enter the beautiful American venues through the kitchen as they were not allowed to enter through the front door even though Duke Ellington and his Orchestra were highly respected and famous worldwide. They traveled, performing throughout Europe, to rave reviews and celebrity treatment, but they were not treated well in their own country, America. This was true for all of the African American entertainers that were so instrumental in molding American culture during the early- to mid-20th century. These entertainers were subject to the same shameful Jim Crow laws that affected every other African American living in America at that time.

Kay had a privileged upbringing since her father was a successful doctor. Though she had come from an affluent background, this type of racial discrimination was nothing new for her or for any other African American of that era. During all of the years that Kay studied at Northwestern University, she was never allowed to live on campus. She and her African American roommate had to rent a room in a Black-owned rooming house in Evanston, Illinois. Kay and her roommate were both musicians studying in the music department. They were the only African American students in the music department at that time, and they were not allowed to use the practice rooms at their discretion. Instead, they were required to practice late at night after all of the White students were finished practicing. It has always been amazing and wonderful to me to see how African Americans, during those very difficult and horrible times in this country, were still able to band together, provide opportunity for each other, have a good time, and make a huge impact on American culture, as well as the culture of the entire world. This is an exemplary case of making lemonade from very bitter lemons. It speaks volumes about the African American spirit – past, present and future.

Kay Davis sang many songs with the Duke Ellington Orchestra, but two of my favorites are "Transblucency" and "Creole Love Call." Kay Davis and composer/pianist Billy Strayhorn gave the very first performance of Strayhorn's *Lush Life* on November 13, 1948 at Carnegie Hall.

Kay is a legendary singer, a wonderful woman and a fantastic mother-in-law. She has shared many wonderful stories with me about her performing experiences, and she has given me a truly unique perspective on this business. Edward, my son, is proud to play his Grammy Kay's songs for his friends on his iPod. That's very cool!

Even in light of the rampant racism in America at that time, Kay has told me fascinating stories about the fun that they had traveling the world performing great music. During the years that she sang with the Duke Ellington Orchestra, several notable musicians were also with the band, including saxophonist, Johnny Hodges; violinist, Ray Nance; and pianist/composer, Billy Strayhorn. Male vocalist Al Hibbler was also with the band from 1943 to 1951. He had several hits with Duke, including "Do Nothing 'Til You Hear From Me," which reached number six on the Billboard Pop Chart and number one on the Harlem Hit Parade. He won the *Down Beat Award* for Best Band Vocalist in 1949. After Hibbler left the band in 1951, he went on to have another huge hit entitled "Unchained Melody" which reached number three on the U.S. Pop Chart. Hibbler's recording of the song preceded that of the Righteous Brothers.

For the last 50 years, Kay has thrown lavish New Year's Eve parties, and Al Hibbler was in attendance at a number of those parties. The first time I met Al Hibbler, my mother was visiting for the Christmas holidays, and Kay asked us to pick him up and bring him to the New Year's Eve party. Upon hearing the news that we'd be in the company of Al Hibbler, my mother was elated. She remembered Hibbler from his many successful recordings. Ed, my mother and I stopped by his sister's home in Chicago where he was spending the holidays. We had a wonderful evening hearing thrilling stories from Al, Kay and several of the other former Duke Ellington Orchestra members. Also present at this party was singer Etta Moten Barnett. Etta had played the signature role of Bess in the 1942 Broadway revival of *Gershwin's Porgy and Bess*. Also among the party guests was the great cabaret artist Bobby Short. It was a wonderful evening and a fabulous way to ring in the New Year!

In addition to Kay Davis, there were two other female singers with the

Duke Ellington Orchestra during those years. Joya Sherrill (1924-2010) was a singer with the Duke Ellington Orchestra from 1944 to 1946. After leaving the orchestra, she toured with several bandleaders, including Benny Goodman. She also took a role in the Broadway musical, *The Long Dream,* before returning to sing with Duke Ellington in 1963. During the 1970's and 80's Joya hosted children's television shows in New York and in the Middle East.

Maria Ellington was the third female singer with the band. Though her last name was Ellington, Maria was not related to Duke. To assure that there was no confusion, Duke introduced her simply as "The Great Marie." As it turned out, Marie went on to marry the legendary Nat King Cole and is the mother of singer Natalie Cole.

Kay and Maria both live in the Central Florida area and have continued to have a close friendship throughout the years. In recent years, they have traveled to Europe together. They enjoy spending time with each other and reminiscing about the old days with Duke's band. Kay shared a story with me about the time in 1948 when Nat King Cole purchased a home in the all White Hancock Park neighborhood of Los Angeles. When members of the property-owner's association told Nat that they didn't want any "undesirables" moving in, Nat replied "Neither do I, and if I see any undesirables coming in, I'll be the first to complain." The Ku Klux Klan was still quite active in the Los Angeles area at that time, and they responded by placing a burning cross in his front yard.

Kay left the Duke Ellington Orchestra in 1950 to marry my father-in law, Edward D. Wimp. They married on July 31, 1950. Edward D. Wimp was a Lieutenant Colonel in the Army. For 35 years, he had a career with the Illinois Department of Revenue, where he was Chief of the Audit Division. He later became a successful real estate broker. Early in his life, in 1932, Edward D. Wimp became the first Black ROTC Cadet to be commissioned at the University of Illinois at Urbana, where he received a bachelor's degree.

Edward

In 1989, Ed and I were blessed with the birth of our only child Edward. Edward was very much awaited as we had been married for several years before his arrival. During his early childhood, our family traveled quite a bit as I performed my shows across America and the world. Due to my work, Edward had early exposure to many people and cultures. Once he began school, the traveling decreased significantly and became limited to winter breaks and summer vacations. It was important to me to be with my family on a daily basis, and I wanted to instill in Edward the values that our family found important. I wanted to read him bedtime stories and to be a member of his school's Mother's Club and attend parent teacher conferences and be at every baseball game. I didn't want to have to make excuses to my child for not being available to support him in every way. My mother shared this bit of advice on several occasions: "For everything that's gained, there's something lost." I found this to be true as I became a mother. I had gained a beautiful child, who is the treasure of my life, but through that acquisition, I had lost the desire to put my interests first. I no longer was comfortable traveling and performing all the time. I wanted to revel in the joys of motherhood. I wanted to build a relationship with my child that would provide a strong foundation to last him a lifetime.

From the time that Edward was very young, we hosted exchange students from around the world. Edward attended the University of Chicago Laboratory Schools through sixth grade. For seventh grade through high school, he attended Morgan Park Academy, a private independent day school in Chicago. Through opportunities made available at Morgan Park Academy, Edward was an exchange student himself, traveling to England, France, Germany, and

Mexico. During his freshman year in high school, Edward attended Sutton Valence Boarding School in Sutton Valence, Kent, England. While there, he was a Cadet in the Royal Air Force (RAF) which is similar to the R.O.T.C. in America. He also played the position of goalie on the Sutton Valence Rugby team.

Ed and I have tried to give Edward opportunities to experience all of the exciting and positive things that the world has to offer. Edward was on the honor roll and he was the captain of both his high school golf and baseball teams. His graduating class consisted of forty-five students, and the small size has allowed him to continue to maintain friendships with his high school contemporaries, as well as with his high school teachers and administrators. Edward has grown up to be a wonderful young man and is currently a student majoring in Business and Political Science at a small private college in Illinois. In addition to being an academic success, his is also a leader in his fraternity and on his college campus. Ed and I are very proud of Edward and his many outstanding accomplishments.

During Edward's formative years, my father-in-law became ill and unable to run his real estate business. My husband was very busy with his McDonald's franchises, so I went to school to get a real estate broker's license, as well as an insurance broker's license since the company also sold insurance. I became President and CEO of DEW Realty Group, Incorporated. We were primarily in the business of property management and property and casualty insurance, though we did sell real estate as well. This business was the perfect solution for me. I wanted to be at home, but I needed intellectual stimulation during the day while Edward was in school. Boy, did I get stimulation! DEW Realty challenged me in many ways. While I was familiar with the concept of management, I was not experienced in dealing with office staff, tenants, workmen, and building mechanicals. I was a small, soft-spoken young woman, and I'm sure that everyone was wondering what in the would I was doing managing them.

My office staff consisted of an office manager, a secretary, two real estate agent/property managers, an insurance agent, and a lawyer. The company managed more than 100 units, sold real estate, and sold lots of insurance. It was tough going at first, but I soon got the hang of it, gaining the respect of the office staff, the workmen, and the tenants. I learned a lot about construction as we were always remodeling and repairing vintage buildings in Chicago.

During my years at DEW Realty, my family and I would travel occasionally as I performed on cruise ships and for corporate events. Mrs. Smith, my office manager, was very smart, experienced, and competent. I would call into the office from destinations across the world, and she would give me a complete rundown of events that had occurred in my absence. She would ask my advice on things and carry out my wishes. Mrs. Smith was single-handedly responsible for me being able to continue occasional touring.

After a decade at the helm of Dew Realty Group, Edward was entering high school. I could see light at the end of the tunnel. I decided to sell the realty business and began preparing to pursue, once again, a full-time performing career. I wanted to have the time to re-establish contacts and be ready to travel and perform full-time once Edward graduated high school and went off to college. I also entered a program of study to receive a Ph.D. in Business Management. I had begun studies toward a Ph.D. many years before and had always promised myself that I would complete that degree. The Chicago Public Schools contacted me during that time about being a consultant to the schools, and I agreed to serve as a consultant, and I have continued to be available the Chicago Public Schools in that capacity.

Edward graduated from high school in June of 2008. Ironically, the autumn of 2008 marked the beginning of the economic recession in America and the world. Many businesses were severely impacted and the entertainment business really took a blow. Top-notch musicians were unable to find work. It was a very difficult time and everyone was hurting. As a result of the contacts and relationships that I had cultivated through the years, I was able to work regularly during the tough recession. I wasn't always getting the caliber of work that I wanted, but at least I was working.

Cultural Exchange

I have always been curious about and interested in other cultures. It is my belief that people the world over basically want the same things. They want to be able to provide a good life for themselves and their families, they want to be respected and they want to live peacefully. I serve as a member of the Board of Directors for *WorldChicago*. WorldChicago, a 501(c) non-profit organization, provides the local community with a unique opportunity to build business relationships and lasting friendships with visitors from around the world. We help enable a better understanding of all cultures, and we help promote Chicago as a vibrant center for commerce, culture, and tourism.

Through the years, I have developed a real love and knowledge of jazz and other types of traditional American music. I also have a great love for world music. My repertoire includes songs in eleven different languages, which allows me to reach out to people no matter where I am performing in the world. Through learning and performing songs in other languages, I get a glimpse into the cultures from which the music comes. Music is truly an international language. It allows musicians to come together and share bits of themselves with each other, often bringing about new musical styles through the fusion of different traditional styles. This is magical.

I currently work regularly with pianist Branislav (Bane) Djordjevic and accordionist Adis Sirbubalo. Both of these musicians have an incredible knowledge of Balkan, Russian, Middle-Eastern, and Asian musical styles. We are fusing this traditional music, which is hundreds--perhaps thousands of years old, with American jazz. It's a wonderful genre called *Gipsy Jazz*. I also have a friend named Greg Duncan who is a very fine jazz trumpeter. He has recently returned from Barcelona, Spain, where he collaborated with musicians in creating *Flamenco Jazz*. Marshall Vente is another pianist and band leader that I work with, performing *Brazilian* music of composers like Antonio Carlos Jobim, Ivan Lins and Sergio Mendes. I am also working with my friend and colleague Dr. Zvonimir Tot, a wonderful guitarist and faculty member at the University of Illinois at Chicago (UIC). We are developing a program of *Fado* music, which is Portuguese folk music featuring voice and guitar. Music is a wonderful way to foster understanding and collaboration between cultures and peoples of the world.

I host and produce a radio show called *Jazz and More with Greta Pope!* The show gives me an opportunity to share the traditional music that I love with my listeners, and it features the music of Louis Armstrong, Ella Fitzgerald, Edith Piaf, Buena Vista Social Club, Nat King Cole, Peggy Lee, Bobby Short, Gipsy Kings, Frank Sinatra, Michael Buble, Nora Jones, Ben Folds, and many, many others. I share interesting facts about the artists, the songs, and the songwriters. Every *Jazz and More!* edition also features the "Joy in the Journey Spotlight Segment," which is an interview with a fascinating person sharing their life journey. *Jazz and More with Greta Pope!* features three of my original compositions as theme music. I have had many guests from around the world on the show, including Duke Ellington vocalist Kay Davis; Maia Baratashvili, a terrific jazz singer from the Republic of Georgia; Noshir Mody, an Indian fusion jazz guitarist; Roger Cairns, a Scottish jazz crooner; and Jabari McDavid, merchandise manager for the internationally acclaimed band, Earth Wind and Fire, just to mention a few. Many of my listeners tune in online. The show enjoys a robust American, as well as an international, listenership.

I love touring and have been a touring entertainer for most of my years in show business. I am currently doing Concert tours and Book tours. I am also a touring Guest Lecturer at Colleges and Universities across the country. Through the years, I have had some very interesting experiences on the road. On one occasion, I was performing for a private party in a penthouse atop the magnificent Hancock Building in Chicago. At the party, I was approached by a distinguished couple, a Romanian man and woman. They indicated that they were interested in having me perform several concerts in Romania, but they didn't know when this could occur because of the political changes afoot in Romania. Yet before they left for the evening, they found me and told me they would be in touch. I didn't hear anything for quite a while, so I figured that they had changed their minds and there would be no concert. Five years later, though, I received a call letting me know that it was finally time. They told me that I would be performing as a contestant in an International Music Festival and that I would be singing an original composition written by a Romanian Gipsy songwriter. They provided me with an instrumental recording of the song and promised me two airline tickets to Bucharest via New York and Vienna. Within a week, my husband and I were to be on our way to Romania.

The night before Ed and I were scheduled to leave, we were told to meet the Romanian couple at 11:00 p.m. at the Rock N Roll McDonald's parking lot in downtown Chicago. This seemed odd, but we met them. Once there, they gave us a few simple instructions and two airline tickets to Bucharest with lay-overs in New York and Vienna. We were to fly United Airlines to New York, and then connect with a Romanian airline by the name of *Tarom*. Ed immediately said *"Tyrone!* That's the name of the airline!!!?

We were to leave early the next morning so we went home, threw some things into our bags, and got a few hours of sleep. We got up the next morning and headed to Chicago's Midway airport where we were shocked to find that we were at the wrong airport. Our flight would be leaving from O'Hare Airport. We were aghast! The reservationist told us that if we hurried, we might be able to get to O'Hare in time to make the flight. We immediately jumped into a taxi and told the driver that we needed to be on a flight leaving O'Hare within the hour. He looked at his watch, told us to fasten our seatbelts, and off we went. He zipped and darted in and out of traffic, honking his horn and driving like a bat out of hell. We made it in a record thirty minutes. Ed thanked him and gave him a very generous tip as we ran into the airport, checked our bags, got our boarding passes, and sprinted to the gate. The reservationist had already begun to close the gate and do her final paperwork before departure. We explained that we had gone to the wrong airport and that this was our connecting flight to Europe and that we had risked life and limb to get here from Midway Airport in time for this flight. She let the flight crew know that we were desperate, and they very kindly allowed us to board. It was the beginning of an adventure I shall never forget.

Romania

We landed in New York City at about noon. Upon our arrival, we began looking for Tarom, the Romanian airline that we were to fly for the rest of our trip. Yet we were unable to find it after a thorough search. We asked at several of the airline desks, but no one seemed to know anything about it. Finally, we asked at the Lufthansa desk and were happy to find out that the Tarom Airlines boarded from their gate, but that they weren't there yet. We couldn't understand how the airline couldn't be there yet--but we didn't say a word. Instead, we went to a bank of seats and made ourselves comfortable, and we waited. And waited, and waited.

The Tarom Flight was to leave New York at 4:30 p.m. At about 3:45, I went up to the desk again to ask about the airline. The woman once again told me that she didn't know what time the representative would arrive. I went back to my seat and reported to Ed. We sat and waited some more. At about 4:15, a man showed up, took out a small handwritten sign with the word "Tarom" spelled out, and put the sign on an easel on top of the reservation desk.

Well, as you might imagine, we were astounded. After we got over our initial shock, we went up to the desk, asked a few questions about the flight's departure time and destination. We were told that the flight would be leaving later that evening and that the flight would in fact be headed to Bucharest, in addition to several other destinations. Our flight was slated to make its first stop in Vienna, Austria before landing in Bucharest. After we were safely deposited in Bucharest Romania, the flight was to continue on to Tel Aviv, Israel; Istanbul, Turkey; Cairo, Egypt; and Athens, Greece.

This all sounded thrilling to me, though I'm not sure what Ed was thinking at this point. Clearly he had reservations about this entire trip. After all, the trip had come up very suddenly – we had been mandated to meet our contacts in a McDonald's parking lot under the cover of darkness the night before the trip, and we didn't even know where Bucharest, Romania was! As if these things were not bizarre enough, we had been waiting all afternoon before finally seeing the little *Tarom* sign at John F. Kennedy International Airport in New York City. Anyone would have been skeptical, but Ed was positive and supportive. We were forging ahead! I am very fortunate to be married to such a wonderful, and courageous guy.

The hours continued to creep by. Again, we waited--and waited--and waited. We were reluctant to even go to the bathroom because no one seemed to know when the flight would be leaving. To add insult to injury, we had been told that if we missed this flight, there would not be another one for two days. So we remained planted in our seats, hoping for any information about this next leg of our trip.

After waiting all afternoon, passengers began to arrive for the Tarom flight at about 8:00 p.m. Ed and I felt a sense of rejuvenation. Within one hour, the Tarom gate area was transformed from a large barren space with two people waiting (Ed and me), to what seemed like a small closet with a *gazillion* people, pushing and shoving to get their place in line. It was unbelievable! We heard many different languages being spoken and smelled many different food smells. We soon realized that there was no food being offered on this flight, so people had brought their own. Again, we were shocked. This was back in the days when food was an expected commodity, certainly on an international flight. Ed immediately went and got us some sandwiches while I held our place in line.

Passengers had very large carry-on suitcases, little children, and shopping bags, along with an array of other various and sundry items. One guy had a staff – a very big stick with a curved top (a lá Little Bo Peep). It was like nothing that I had ever seen before!

The reservationist knew that Ed and I had been patiently waiting for a very long time, so when it became time to actually board the plane, we were allowed to board first. This was very nice and it gave us an opportunity to sit where we wanted, as there was no assigned seating. As we boarded, we could hear loud, somewhat frenetic music playing on the plane. This music seemed like it might cause people to be overly excited, but what did we know? We went ahead and selected our seats and put our small carry-on bag in the overhead bin, sat down and put our seatbelts on. It was dark outside and the lights on the plane were glaring. Soon thereafter, a crush of people rushed onto the plane talking loudly in languages that we couldn't understand. They were grabbing seats, trying to shove large carry-on bags into small overhead bins and bickering with the flight attendants. Ed and I just sat in our seats amazed. We were surely in for the ride of our lives!

Three Hassidic Jewish gentlemen boarded the plane and began looking around for seats. There were three available seats right in front of us, and they came over to the three seats and began what appeared to be praying over the seats. They did this for several minutes and then turned away and selected three seats elsewhere on the plane. Needless to say, this made us a little nervous about the seat selection that we had made, and we couldn't help thinking that maybe they knew something that we didn't.

We also watched a woman board the plane with five little children. She was locating single seats for them, as there were not five available seats together. There was one empty seat next to Ed, and the woman placed a rather rambunctious young boy in that seat. We were certain that this little boy would surely make our lives miserable all the way across the Atlantic. Fortunately, the child began crying for his mother and a very nice older gentleman gave up his seat so that the boy could sit next to her. That very kind man took the seat next to Ed. Whew!

After an hour of this frantic commotion, the plane began backing up and heading for the runway. People were still standing up! The overhead bins were still open. The lights and the music seemed more intense than ever, and the flight attendants were yelling at the top of their lungs. It was pandemonium, but the plane took off.

Once airborne, things began to calm down. The music was turned off and the lights were dimmed. People began to settle-in for the long flight. Ed motioned for the flight attendant to come over so that we could get an estimated arrival time. We were unsure of the time that we would actually arrive at our destination. As a matter of fact, we were unsure of our destination. Ed, ever so kindly, asked the flight attendant what time we would be arriving in Bangladesh.

"Bangladesh!" she cried. "Oh Sir, you're on the wrong flight!" Oops! We soon realized that Ed had said the wrong city − Bangladesh, Budapest, Bucharest − we were so confused!

The flight to Europe was very pleasant and the Tarom crew was wonderful. It later occurred to us that the reason for the confusion was that there was no common language among the passengers and flight crew. People were struggling to understand each other and to understand what was going on. The remaining portion of our trip to Bucharest was uneventful.

We had a very short lay-over in Vienna, and then we were on our way to Bucharest. It was so exciting! As we descended for our landing into Bucharest, we saw soldiers marching up and down the runway. This was not a new sight for me as I had seen this plenty of times during my U.S.O. days. I must say, though, that I wondered why soldiers were marching up and down *this* runway, but I wasn't alarmed. We finally landed and the plane came to a stop in an airfield. Ed and I were immediately escorted from the plane to a waiting limousine. We were taken to a secured private area in the airport where someone took our passports and asked that we sit and wait. Several gentlemen came into the waiting area, introduced themselves, and told us that they were our contacts there. We had been given their names before we left Chicago. One was the producer of the festival, one was a television personality waiting to do an interview with me, and the other was my bodyguard. *Bodyguard*?! Why did I need a bodyguard???

After they returned our passports to us, we got into the limousine and were taken to our hotel. The accommodations were very nice and the people there were very welcoming and kind to us. This was the start of a most enjoyable and informative stay in Bucharest, Romania.

Flowers...and More Flowers!

During our first few days in Romania, we rested and did some sight-seeing. One location that was particularly beautiful was Lake Snagov, which is about 25 to 30 kilometers from Bucharest and the home of the Snagov Monastery. Though we did not see the actual Monastery, we enjoyed a private, very elegant and delicious luncheon alongside the lake. We were serenaded by a string quartet and we enjoyed white tablecloths, beautiful flowers, bone china, white-gloved waiters, and expensive champagne. What more could a girl ask? It was idyllic. We had a lovely afternoon relaxing and hearing about the history of Romania.

Romania is a very beautiful country that had been war ravaged up until several months before our visit in June of 1990. In December of 1989, Nicolae Ceauscescu, the President of Romania, and his wife had been executed. It had been a very tumultuous time in Romania, and there were still many signs of the recent unrest, including bullet pockmarks on Bucharest's downtown buildings. We were told not to leave our hotel without our armed bodyguard. We did exactly as we were told, and they took very good care of us. Even in light of the difficulties that Romania had endured, the people were optimistic and looking forward to a brighter day. I am always amazed by how resilient the human spirit is. No matter where you are in the world, no matter how tough things are, the majority of people have kindness in their hearts. We were met with nothing but love during our stay in Bucharest.

On the day of my first rehearsal with the band that I'd be working with, I was very impressed by the level of musicianship. These guys were fantastic! They had studied classical technique extensively from childhood, so they were great with the classical repertoire. They were wonderful sight-readers and very sensitive players. What was really surprising to me was how adept they were at the jazz repertoire. They knew all of the jazz greats and could mimic their playing styles. The pianist, named Ciprian, did not speak English well, but he could play very well in a style reminiscent of the great American jazz pianist Art Tatum. It was quite fantastic. At one very special moment, we looked at each other, both wanting to communicate, but language was a barrier. So Ciprian began playing "As Time Goes By" from the great 1942 American film *Casablanca* with Humphrey Bogart and Ingrid Bergman. I was astounded that he knew the song, but I happily sang along with him. That beautiful song allowed Ciprian and me to communicate with each other and express our deep regard for each other as musicians and as people. It was a very special and moving exchange.

Finally, the big day arrived. We were well rehearsed and ready for my Romanian debut. I was performing for the newly created music festival that has since become known as EUROPAfest. The festival features instrumentalists and vocalists from more than 40 countries around the world. The contestants compete and a winner is chosen. As a result of my performance before 7000 audience members, I won this competition. My performance was aired on national Romanian television, and I became very well known throughout Romania.

On the evening that I won the competition, the band, the producers, and many others involved with the performance, along with all of our spouses, went to a beautiful restaurant in Bucharest. The restaurant had already closed for the evening, but they were more than happy to open up, especially for us as we celebrated our victory at the festival. We had an absolute blast − eating, dancing, playing music, laughing, and thoroughly enjoying each other's company. The sun was coming up when we were leaving. Needless to say, it was an enchanting night that I will never forget.

As we left the restaurant and got into the limousine, I noticed that people were lining the streets. I asked if they were waiting for the buses on their way to work. The producer told me that they were there to catch a glimpse of me. I couldn't believe it! I was a celebrity in Romania!!! People waved and cried as the limousine passed, making its way back to the hotel. It was unbelievable and very humbling.

When we arrived back at the hotel, we found a huge pile of cut flowers, about four feet high, filling the entire sitting room. They were beautiful and fragrant. It is the custom in Romania to throw flowers at a performer that you like. Everyone in the audience had flowers and they had thrown them onto the stage during my performance. The producers had been kind enough to gather the flowers and take them to my hotel suite. It was lovely.

Yes, that maiden trip to Romania was fantastic. The following year I returned to Romania as the previous winner and as the English speaking television commentator for the international broadcast of the festival. I had a great time, made many wonderful friends, and created incredible memories to last a lifetime.

As a post-script to this story, several years later I was taking the course of study to allow me to work with Ed in the McDonald's business. I was studying to become a McDonald's Owner Operator and was attending a class at McDonald's Hamburger University in Oak Brook, Illinois. The class consisted of about fifty students, many of whom were from other countries. On the first day of class, everyone had to stand up and introduce themselves. There was a man in the class from Romania. During a class break, I approached the man, welcoming him to America and letting him know that I had been to his country twice. He couldn't believe it. He asked why I had been there, and when I told him that I had participated in the festival there, he responded in his thick Romanian accent, *"Greta Pope!!!"*

Tiny Bubbles

On another occasion, I was traveling to Hawaii with a production for an industrial show. Industrial shows are performances in which original song lyrics are created for corporate conventions to reinforce the corporate message to their employees. Often, awards are given to high achievers during the course of the convention, which generally lasts for several days. I have performed industrial shows for many corporate clients in many locations.

There is one specific industrial show that I recall as if it were yesterday. We were headed to Maui to do a show for a major American insurance company. This was a very big contract and our entire crew was very excited. We rehearsed the show with our cast of six performers and five musicians and were finally ready to make the eight hour trip from Chicago to Maui. We would have a brief lay-over in Los Angeles and then we'd be headed to beautiful, sunny Hawaii. The month was January, so we were thrilled for this opportunity to spend a few days in a warm climate. As we were gathering at O'Hare Airport, members of the band were saying goodbye to their spouses and confirming pick-up arrangements for our return to O'Hare ten days later. Rocky, the drummer, kissed his wife goodbye and asked her to take his coat home with the understanding that she would bring it back when she picked him up in ten days. After all, he was going to Hawaii, he wouldn't need it! We boarded the flight and headed to Hawaii.

Maui was absolutely beautiful. The brief, daily afternoon showers produced a stunning palette of lush, green foliage and vividly colorful flowers that were like nothing I had ever seen before. It was magnificent! The weather was perfect and our shows went beautifully. We performed with the fabulous Tony Award winning actress/singer Bernadette Peters. We had an opportunity to spend time off-stage with Peters and her drummer Cubby O'Brien. As it turned out, Cubby O'Brien was "Cubby" from the original 1950's vintage television show *The Mickey Mouse Club*. He was a *Mousketeer!*

All in all, we had a fantastic time. When our shows were finished, it was time to return to Chicago. We had an uneventful trip from Maui to the Big Island and from the Big Island of Hawaii to Los Angeles. We were scheduled for a red-eye flight and we arrived at LAX (Los Angeles International Airport) in plenty of time to get our connecting flight to Chicago. We spent time on the return flight reminiscing about the great time that we'd had on Maui. During the course of the flight, the Captain announced that the weather in Chicago was very cold – twenty below zero to be exact. We had left paradise and were heading for sub-zero temps. *What a drag!!!*

We finally landed in Chicago only to find that it was so cold, cars were not starting. Electricity in some areas was out. People were freezing. It was shocking! Rocky's wife had called his cell phone indicating that their family car would not start and that she would not be able to pick him up from the airport. Worse yet, *she had his coat!* Rocky had arrived at O'Hare Airport in twenty below zero temperatures, wearing a Hawaiian shirt and Panama hat. This was disastrous! How would he get home? This type of weather is so severe, that exposed skin can become frost bitten with the tiniest bit of exposure. Rocky was in trouble.

My husband saved the day with a great idea for getting Rocky home. Ed went and got our SUV from the airport parking lot and turned the heat up to its maximum level. After allowing the vehicle to warm up for half an hour or so, with the sanction and help of airport security, Ed pulled the vehicle up onto the sidewalk and up to the door of the airport. The airport provided blankets and we wrapped Rocky in them and rushed him into our vehicle. We drove him home, where his wife met us in the driveway with his coat, hat, scarf and gloves. Rocky was relieved and grateful to be safely at home. This was an important lesson for us all. Never leave home without seasonally appropriate clothing. You never know what might happen. Always aim to be as prepared as you possibly can.

Côte d'Azur...Oui!

The last touring story that I'll share is about a tour of the Cote d'Azur, or the French Riviera in southern France. I had performed a tour of ten concerts throughout the area with the fantastic 100-piece Northshore Concert Band at beautiful large outdoor venues across southern France. It was a wonderful tour where we met many kind French people who welcomed us with open arms. My family accompanied me on this tour and we had a great time. When the tour was finished, Ed, Edward and I were headed back to Chicago. Our flight was to leave from Nice with a plane change in Munich, Germany before heading to the U.S. on the evening of July 2nd. We were to meet my mother-in-law, Kay on the evening of July 3rd as she was coming to spend our July 4th wedding anniversary with us.

I scheduled our flight thinking that we'd be home in plenty of time to meet Kay at the airport. However, the flight from Nice was delayed for several hours due to mechanical problems and we were forced to wait at the Nice Airport until early evening when the problem was finally taken care of. When we arrived in Munich, we were shocked to find that the last daily flight to the United States had already gone and that we would have to stay overnight in Munich. They provided us with wonderful hotel accommodations, dinner and breakfast. Under ordinary circumstances, we would have been thrilled with this opportunity − it was a great additional night in Europe − but we were unable to really enjoy it because we were panicked about our pending rendezvous with Kay!

I tried calling Kay at her home in Orlando the evening of July 2nd, as she would be leaving early the next morning. Her phone rang and rang and rang, but there was no answer. We knew that she often spent the night preceding a trip at a hotel near the Orlando airport, but we had no idea which hotel. I knew her flight information, so I asked the airline that we were flying to contact the airline that she would be flying to let her know that we would be late coming in. This communication did not happen and Kay arrived in Chicago with no idea of what was going on and no one to meet her. Fortunately, she called a family friend and they were able to pick her up. They were also able to reach us via cell phone to find out where we were. When we finally arrived in Chicago, we were able to spend time with Kay. It was a wonderful visit and a very memorable anniversary. All is well that ends well.

I have had many interesting and exciting touring experiences. Touring is certainly one of the gratifying by-products of being in the entertainment business. There are many opportunities to meet fascinating people and see new things. Touring also teaches artists to be resourceful while navigating their way through interesting and unexpected circumstances. From delayed travel, to incremental weather, to equipment and personnel issues, touring is exciting! It's a great way to share fantastic music, build a fan-base, sell merchandise, and provide an important service to humankind.

I hope that you enjoy this book and that you find great benefit in the ideas shared herein. This book is designed to provide the reader with the basics for building a successful music career. Success in this business is dependent upon many things, including commitment to one's craft, establishing goals, devising a strategy, and employing unrelenting persistence. It is my belief that if we, as musicians, each build our own following, together, we can cultivate a large audience base for ourselves and for each other. We can make intimate live music a preferred type of entertainment for the masses within American culture, as well as world culture. Music experienced in large stadium type venues is great, but there is nothing like enjoying a wonderful artist in an intimate setting where you can feel the warmth of that performer's presence.

It is incumbent upon us as performers to use our art form to enhance the human experience. In this age of impersonal communication and fast living, people long for that human touch. Intimate live music can provide that special connection to help us rekindle the fire in our souls, the love in our hearts, and the gentleness of our spirit that is often missing in our lives.

I wish you all the best in finding your own path to success. Believe in yourself and always, always follow your dreams!

Music, Money & You Seminars and Consulting Services are available to colleges, universities, performing arts high schools, churches, individuals, and music organizations of all types. For information on *Music, Money & You* Seminars and Consulting Services, contact info@gretapope.com or phone 773-965-4200.

I hope that the information shared in this upcoming section of *Music, Money & You: Managing the Business* will make a difference in your life.

Performers attend the finest music conservatories, graduating with degrees in music performance, only to get out into the real world not knowing how to navigate their way. These performers have not been trained to create work for themselves. They expect that a symphony orchestra or an opera company or a record producer will discover them and they will live happily ever after. That happens for some performers, but not for most. I hope that this book will help you to move your career forward.

Chapter 1

What is Entertainment Management?

As a performing artist or manager, you are in the business of entertainment. Entertainment can be defined in many ways.

Entertainment, as defined by Webster's Dictionary, is *"a source or means of amusement, cheer, delight, diversion, enjoyment, frolic, fun, merriment, pastime, pleasure, recreation, and sport. It is pleasure afforded by an amusing act or spectacle. It implies thought and mental occupation, but in an agreeable, refreshing way. The word entertainment is used in terms of mirthful, mental delight."*

Some of the more common forms of entertainment today are music, art, theater, cinema, television and sports to name a few. In more simple terms, entertainment transports us away from our daily cares. It helps us to relax and forget about the stresses of our jobs, family troubles, money woes, health concerns, and many other things. It can take us into an altered state of awareness that helps us cope with daily life.

As we already know, entertainment can take many forms: theater, music, art, literature or sports. Entertainment can also be knitting, quilting, auto repair, auto racing and other such things. Entertainment can be almost anything that provides pleasure to the participant.

What is the function of Entertainment in society?

The function of entertainment is to provide an enjoyable and pleasant diversion from everyday life. Entertainment is a very important component of any society. It is especially important in today's fast-paced, highly-stressed cultures of the world. People need diversions from the pressures of life. Whether they work in the field of education, civil service, medicine, technology, homemaking, law, the arts, government or whatever, everyone needs a break from the "sameness" of a busy life. We need something to make us laugh, as well as to make us feel pride and respect for our fellow human beings and for ourselves. We need something around which we can rally and become unified. Whether it is in the form of sports, movies, live theater, concerts or whatever--we need entertainment!

In order to be successful in the entertainment business, it is important to clearly understand what entertainment is and its importance to people. Quality entertainment evokes emotion and is particularly effective when the participant experiences a wide range of feelings culminating in a moral, prideful, joyful conclusion. This allows the participant or audience member to be truly swept up in the moment, leaving them thoroughly renewed by the entertainment experience.

The public perception of the entertainer is often overly simplified. People view entertainment as fun, because entertainment is generally part of a fun atmosphere. People work all day and perhaps enjoy a movie or concert in the evening when their work is finished. Entertainers are people that provide joy and merriment during those hours of relaxation. It is often not apparent that during the hours of relaxation for most people, the entertainer is working at a craft that they have spent many years developing. They are working at a job that they have been highly trained to perform. Good entertainers have a prescribed approach to their craft. The skilled and successful entertainer takes his/her craft very seriously. Generally, a great deal of study, skill, and talent are all a part of the product offered.

The professional entertainer also takes their obligation to the audience seriously. The audience comes to a performance expecting to be spirited away, through whatever entertainment vehicle that they have chosen. They want to be transported from their day-to-day existence. They want to laugh, to cry, to be amused, and to be made to think about the greater meaning of life. The experienced, professional entertainer meets and exceeds the audience's expectations by giving them a glimpse into their world through sharing their talent, their persona, and their enthusiasm.

Though there are many types of entertainment, this book will deal exclusively with the type of entertainment provided by the live performing artist or entertainer. An audience's expectations of an entertainer are great; and great entertainers respect, understand, and meet those expectations. A great entertainer presents material that fans can relate to, in a manner that is simple and sincere. The entertainer reveals him/herself to be a likable human being-- the guy/girl next door. During their performances and public appearances, they allow the audience to feel familiar with them, as though they are good friends. They may share stories about their experiences or their family, allowing the audience to identify with them.

A great deal of time and study goes into deciding how a good relationship with an audience will be achieved. It is difficult as an artist, to view oneself objectively and for this reason, entertainers seek outside input to develop what is called a "stage persona." Of course sincerity and believability is crucial, so the "stage persona" must be very well thought out and is often most successful when it's an exaggeration of the best features of the artist's actual personality and appearance. A Manager, an objective person, assists in identifying and magnifying that artist's best features. This manager will also work with the artist and help to develop the artist into a marketable "product." The product, once fully developed will consist of the "stage persona," which includes wardrobe, hair style, material performed, manner of speaking and many other things. So, it is becoming increasingly clear that good entertainment is created, crafted and prescribed--down to the tiniest detail. Very little is left to chance.

Though entertainers appear to be having fun, they are working very hard, not only at the moment of performance, but behind the scenes as well. A good entertainer understands that entertainment is a business. Without hard work and a distinct business plan, success on every level will be elusive. A great deal more work goes into creating a successful entertainment product than is often times credited. Yes, the perception of entertainment is fun, but the fact is that entertainment is not only a business, it is a *tough* business. In order for all components of an entertainment product to work together successfully, they must be expertly managed, hence the need for Entertainment Management.

What is Entertainment Management?

Entertainment Management is a business discipline through which entertainment of all types is developed, controlled, and made available to the public. The term to manage, according to Webster's Dictionary, means *"to direct or conduct the affairs or business of a person, place or thing."*

Entertainment Management can relate to the management of entertainment facilities such as cinema, live theater, live music venues, theme parks, sports events, and nightclubs. Entertainment Management can also refer to the management of art galleries, broadcast media companies, and museums. In good economic times people want to spend their money on various types of recreational activities, many of which would be categorized as entertainment. In bad economic times people still spend on recreational activities, but they are more selective. In either scenario, they are looking for quality experiential entertainment options for themselves and for their friends and families.

In order to cover all of the areas of application for Entertainment Management many courses of study would be required. The business discipline of Entertainment Management is a very broad field. Pursuing this rigorous course of study prepares a student, through careful inspection of all of the aspects of the Business, to work successfully in the expansive field of Entertainment Management. *Music, Money & You: Managing the Business,* along with the associated college level course, entitled *Introduction to Artist Management 101; the Business of Entertainment* is designed to fulfill one aspect of study as a student works toward the Bachelor Degree in Business or Performing Arts. In this book we will deal solely with Management of the "live performing artist." For the purpose of this study, the term Entertainment Management will refer to the management of the individual or group that is the "entertainer, artist, or live performer." For our purposes, this is the "product."

How this book will help you...the Performing Artist?

Through many years of working with musicians and performers, the one thing that I have heard repeatedly from them is "I am not getting the amount or type of work that I want. I just don't know how to market myself!" My response to them is always the same: I share with them a few methods that I have found to be effective for creating work and invariably they tell me, "I don't have the time to do all of that!" I certainly understand their position. Being a performing artist is a full-time job. It requires daily practice and study. A musician/performer must have time to learn new music and continually improve their skills in order to be on the cutting edge of the business. And, if they do not have the funds to put an effective team in place, they also must effectively market and promote themselves.

Musicians and performing artists go to school to master their craft. Many of them go on for graduate degrees, seeking to further perfect their technique. While some musicians choose to work in the field of music education at the primary, secondary or college levels, most musicians want to make their living playing music. The love of music and performing are the things that initially caused them to pursue a career in music. Unfortunately, in order to make ends meet, many performing artists find themselves having to take on a "day gig" or an alternate type of employment unrelated to music. Many talented, trained musicians and performers have experienced great disappointment in having to give up their dream of professionally making music. This is truly unfortunate, because with a little help, they could work successfully in the field. *Music, Money & You!...Managing the Business* is designed to help the talented and prepared performing artist understand how to take control of their career and find success. The first step is for the artist to view him or herself as the entertainment "product."

The Product

Entertainment Management is the discipline that connects the entertainer, or product, successfully with the public. Entertainment Management also connects the entertainer with all of the entities and services needed to have a successful career in the field of entertainment. Success, as defined in this book means that the talented, well-prepared performing artist will be able to work and make a good living wage in the entertainment field. Of course finding success is contingent upon working hard, working smart, and being organized. Often, performing artists think that being a "star" is the only way to have success in the entertainment business. This is simply not true. Yes, it is true that some artists will find fame and fortune, but those artists are few and far between. It is possible to make a good living in the entertainment business without being a household name. I have many friends, who, by 1.) finding their personal niche, 2.) being available to go where the work is and 3.) working tirelessly; have been able to make a great deal of money as entertainers without being household names. Two of my personal friends that come immediately to mind are entertainer/comic/composer Billy Fellows; and entertainer/singer/trumpeter Greg Bonham. Along with many other performers that I've worked with, these guys are both are very hard-working and committed to being successful. I have spent a great deal of time with each of these gentlemen on the road performing for all kinds of events. They tour performing for private corporate events, as well as working Las Vegas and Atlantic City. They do very well in the entertainment business. Comedian/ventriloquist Jeff Dunham is another performer with whom I have worked extensively. He has had tremendous success, though you may not recognize his name.

The performing artist must take his/her career in hand and move it forward. Depending upon the artist's level in the business, this can be done in several ways.

The Beginning Artist

An artist starting off in the business will not have much money coming in from their business, and for that reason will probably need to be more "hands on" with their career. The beginning artist can most effectively benefit from this book by reading, understanding, and personally implementing the management techniques found herein. This will take a great deal of time, but for the committed artist it will be time well spent.

The Advanced Artist

By the time an artist has begun to develop a following; is getting work; and has money coming in, it often becomes difficult for them to find the time to handle the day-to-day details of their career. If they are working regularly and/or touring, they will most likely need a Manager to handle the day-to-day tasks which will be discussed in the next few chapters. The scope of this part of my book will address the needs of the beginning artist as well as those of the advanced artist.

We will consider the entertainment management business through the eyes of the individual wishing to function in the role of the Manager. This approach will give aspiring managers valuable guidance, in addition to guiding performing artists, either by helping them to manage their own careers or by helping them to know what to look for when they're ready to engage a Manager.

From the Manager's Perspective

Through the many components of entertainment management, an artist's needs can be met in every way. Entertainment Management entails many things, the first of which is selecting an artist or "product" with which to work. Product selection will be discussed in great detail in the next chapter. Once selected, the artist/product needs development. After the artist/product has been developed, the manager then goes on to build a "brand" for the artist/product.

What is a Brand?

There are many schools of thought regarding the term "Brand" or "Branding."

The Oxford Dictionary of Business and Management defines a brand as:

"a name, sign or symbol used to identify items or services of the seller(s) and to differentiate them from goods of competitors."

Signs and symbols are part of what a brand is, but to us this is a very incomplete definition.

Walter Landor, one of the greats of the advertising industry, said:

"Simply put, a brand is a promise. By identifying and authenticating a product or service it delivers a pledge of satisfaction and quality."

In his book "Building Strong Brands" David Aaker suggests the brand is a ëmental box' and defines brand equity as:

"A set of assets (or liabilities) linked to a brand's name and symbol that adds to (or subtracts from) the value provided by a product or service--" A brand is the most valuable real-estate in the world, a corner of the consumer's mind."

As is mentioned in David Aaker's definition, brands are not necessarily positive. When building a brand, one must take into consideration the consumers experience with the business entity from beginning to end. So, it is clear that "branding" is very important to the public's perception of any product. A good manager must have an objective eye regarding the "product" so that "branding" can begin. The manager works to build a reputation, fan base, following and audience for the product/artist.

In addition to building the artist's brand, the manager also takes steps to provide good legal counsel, to provide an agent, accountants, and venues for performance, along with handling stage lighting, sound, security, transportation etc. Everything pertaining to the entertainer is managed through the discipline of Entertainment Management.

What is an Entertainment Manager?

The Entertainment Manager, sometimes referred to as a Manager or Personal Manager, manages an artist similarly to the way a Corporate Manager manages a product, brand or service. He or she is a personal representative of the artist, working very closely with the artist. This individual plays an important role in artist development. The Entertainment Manager can be vital to the success or failure of an artist. Entertainment Managers advise and counsel artists on virtually all aspects of a performing career. Through a very careful interview and observation process, the Manager identifies a viable product (artist). The Manager then gets to know the artist professionally and personally, thereby gaining the knowledge and insight necessary to further develop that product. When the product is fully developed to the Manager's satisfaction, the Manager then promotes and markets that product to the public.

The very first step is artist selection.

Chapter 2

"Product" or Artist Selection

Based on the Entertainment Manager's experience and research, they generally use three ways to locate clients:

through referrals from others in the business such as record label executives, publishers, booking agents, producers, entertainment lawyers, accountants, etc.

through existing clients

through discovery by scouting clubs, recording studios, the internet, etc.

Careful consideration of all aspects of the selection is very important. The Manager must first be able to relate to and understand the artist's musical style. If the artist is a punk rocker and the perspective Manager is a fan of Classical music, the relationship might not be very productive for either of them. The Manager would very likely not know what steps would be necessary to appeal to the artist's following or audience. He or she would probably not have the knowledge, passion, or enthusiasm necessary to market the artist effectively. It is important that the artist's style, values, and goals be compatible with those of the Manager.

Style -- The Manager's style should be compatible with the artist's style. For example; if the artist appeals to an audience with traditional musical tastes, it would be important for the Manager to have some knowledge of that style and for the Manager to have some contacts with venues and recording labels that promote that style of music.

Values -- Values are an important part of the manager/artist relationship. Hopefully, over the long term, the Manager and Artist will become great friends as they spend endless hours together building a successful career. A personal understanding and common ideas of social values is helpful. If the manager is working with a Christian Music artist, it would not be good for him/her to be a heavy drinker or avid gambler. These vices would probably not be compatible with the artist's values or with those of the artist's following.

Goals -- There are many definitions of success in this business. It's important that the Manager and artist have the same end result in mind and understand the goals toward which they are working. The manager may want to develop an International act that travels worldwide for three months of the year, takes three months off and works the other six months in Las Vegas. The artist may have a family or other obligations and may want to live full time in Los Angeles, seek film/TV work and not travel at all. This kind of discrepancy in the business goals of these two individuals will make working together very difficult. The Manager and Artist must first and foremost share the same goals.

The Manager must be comfortable working with the Artist. He or she must understand the artist's lifestyle, family commitments, talent level, entertainment experience, attitude toward the business, along with many other things. Only after having several honest, heart-to-heart conversations should the Manager and Artist even consider entering into a relationship.

Many managers start off as a long-time friend to the artist before even thinking about functioning in the role of Manager. One relationship that I am aware of began as a friendship 15 years before it became a manager/artist relationship. Melvin, a Blues singer/guitarist, and Mike, a car salesman for an auto dealership, have been friends for many years. Melvin and Mike were sharing their dissatisfaction with the progress of their respective careers. Melvin had been singing and playing for many years in taverns and night clubs around his hometown. He wanted new and more lucrative challenges, but had not been able to realize his dreams. Mike had been working all of his adult life as a used car salesman. While he was happy with the money that he was making, he felt stalled in a job where there wasn't much room for growth. He also wanted a new challenge.

The two friends decided to collaborate, Melvin with his exceptional musical talents and Mike with his long-time sales experience. Their business relationship has proven very successful. With Mike on his team Melvin is working constantly, across the Nation and abroad. He has made several recordings and regularly opens for major artists. Melvin and Mike are continuing to seek more lucrative work. Together they've come a long way from the local tavern and the used car lot. They are friends, business partners, have the same goals in mind, and are experiencing great success.

The Entertainment Manager, with the input of the artist, must create vision, goals, and objectives for the future of the artist. The Manager must also realize that his/her own future in this business is dependent upon their ability to effectively manage the artist, generate interest in the artist, and build the artist's brand. This individual must manage all of the many outside forces with which the artist will come in contact.

What Should A Manager Look For In An Artist?

The ideal artist is one that has a high level of commitment to their career. They are determined to be successful in the business. It is, of course, important to ask whether the artist has the following attributes:

Talent

Is the artist trained and experienced in their craft (vocal or instrumental)?

Desire

Is success in the music business a top priority for the artist?

Belief

Does the artist believe that they have what it takes to make it?

Good personality

Is the artist easy to work with and likable?

Hard working

Is the artist resilient? An artist must be willing to work very hard to attain success. He or she must also be willing to accept constructive criticism and make positive changes. He or she should not be deterred by disappointment. There is a great deal of rejection in the entertainment business. The artist must learn to view him or herself objectively. It's important to continue to press ahead.

Business-like

Entertainment is a business. Being on time and prepared is key. An artist must be disciplined and act appropriately in all situations. There is no room for difficult personalities. Many aspiring artists have found doors of opportunity closing for them the moment word gets around that they are a "problem" to work with.

Positive attitude

An artist must believe that they will be successful in the entertainment business and be willing to work tirelessly to achieve their goals.

The manager should look for an artist who is being him or herself and is original. The manager should also determine which of the three management alternatives is appropriate for the artist:

Self Management

--suited for an artist who is just starting out, needs additional experience, and has no income.

Limited Management

--suited for a working artist who still has the time to deal with many aspects of his/her business, such as bill paying, securing engagements, etc.

Total Management

--suited for the artist who is very busy and doesn't have the time to tend to the day-to-day operational aspects of his/her business.

The manager must discuss goals, motivation and needs with the artist. It's important for the artist to get a clear picture of the manager's background and it is equally important for the manager to verify background information about the artist.

Some of the questions to be asked of the artist by the manager are:

- What are your career goals and objectives?
- Where do you want to go with your career?
- Do you want to place more emphasis on recording?
- Do you want to concentrate on personal appearances?
- Do you want to spend time writing songs?
- Do you want to focus on all of the aforementioned areas?

A good manager should become a member of professional organizations in the field. There are several organizations of this type. One that comes to mind is the *Council of Personal Managers.* He/she should also be listed in the *Billboard International Talent and Touring Directory.* Affiliations such as these filter information from viable sources and help the manager to be on the cutting edge of industry trends.

Education and personal demeanor is also an important aspect of functioning well as a personal manager. Being able to communicate easily with others, to express one's self orally, and to write on many levels is crucial. A college degree and some experience in business and/or law are extremely helpful in this business.

Chapter 3

So You've Found Your Artist--Now What?

I cannot stress the importance of exercising caution in establishing the Manager/Artist relationship. Many Artists do not have the personal fortitude to ever be successful in the business. Some are not disciplined while others might have issues that will make them difficult to work with.

Once a suitable artist has been located, the manager should take plenty of time in the courtship phase with this artist. It has been shown time and time again that the longer the courtship before a marriage, the more successful the marriage is likely to be. The same is true with the artist/manager relationship. A level of mutual commitment and trust must be established. The artist and manager must be on the same wavelength. Each must totally trust and have faith in the other. It is advisable to schedule a preliminary exploratory conference.

The Preliminary Exploratory Conference

As has been previously discussed, the artist and manager will need to come to an agreement as to what type of management relationship will be most suitable. This is generally determined through a Preliminary Exploratory Conference which gives the artist and manager an opportunity to accumulate necessary information to determine the type of relationship that will be established. The information gathered during this conference will be the basis of the Management Agreement. The preliminary exploratory conference is not for negotiating the management contract. It is a data gathering session to determine the feasibility of entering into a contract. The discussion may include asking whether or not the artist is married, has a family, or is committed to a personal relationship and how these relationships might affect a full-fledged music career. How does the spouse feel about the possibility of the artist leaving the family to perform concerts on the road? What are the artist's thoughts and plans regarding how a music career would fit into his/her life?

The preliminary exploratory conference should also include things such as:

- Artist's personal goals
- Artist's career history
- Artist's financial condition (professionally and personally)
- Does artist have an accountant?
- Does artist have an attorney?
- Does artist have life insurance? Vehicle insurance?
- Are there debts or financial obligations?
- Are there other outstanding contractual agreements with:
- *Record companies?*
- *Publishers?*
- *Agents?*
- *Other managers?*
- Why did this artist come to you for management?
- Were they referred by a record label?
- Has artist ever been signed to a big record deal?
- Has the artist just been dropped from a major label?

It cannot be said enough, check the artist's background. Know who you're dealing with.

Other things that you'll want to know are:

- *What legal entity is the artist doing business as:*
- *Sole proprietor?*
- *Partnership?*
- *Limited liability company?*
- *Corporation?*
- *Joint venture?*

Ownership must be established, especially where the artist is a duo or group.

- Are there existing management, booking, recording, publishing or corporate endorsement or sponsorship agreements in effect?
- What are the terms of those agreements?
- What is the artist's status with regard to parties to those agreements?
- If agreements are expired, etc. are there proper releases?
- What are the artist's professional assets?

Is the artist a member of applicable unions such as:

- AFTRA -- American Federation of Television and Radio Artists?
- AGVA -- American Guild of Variety Artists?
- AFM -- American Federation of Musicians?
- AEA -- Actors Equity Association?
- SAG -- Screen Actors Guild?
- Other professional organizations?

- What is the artist's personal and business debt structure?
- Does the artist own a registered servicemark on his/her name?
- What is the artist's reputation and current image?
- What kind of exposure and experience has the artist had as a live performer?
- What is the artist's earning history?

- Have proper financial records been kept?
- Are there good banking relationships?
- Have proper Federal and State income tax returns been filed for the last five years?
- Is there proper insurance coverage?
- Does the artist write his/her own material?
- Is the artist a member of a performing rights society?
- Who controls and administers the artist's copyrighted musical compositions?
- Does the artist have any affiliate companies (publishing or production)?
- What is the artist's past recording experience?
- What industry trends might have an effect on the artist's career?

The manager should also consider the following questions which are absolutely crucial to longevity and success of the relationship.

- Are the manager and artist compatible?
- Is the artist willing to work toward the stated goals or does he/she expect the manager to do everything?
- Is the artist realistic?
- Does the artist have the ability and discipline to face the hard times as well as the good times?
- Is the artist dependable?
- What is the artist's reputation in the industry?

The Preliminary Exploratory Conference gives both the artist and manager an opportunity to evaluate each other's talent, personality, and capabilities. Once these questions have been answered to the manager's satisfaction, as well as the artist's satisfaction a sound decision can be made as to whether or not pursuing the artist/manager relationship is feasible. If the answer of both parties is yes, then it is time to move forward.

How Is The Manager Paid?

Managers are usually paid a commission based on the gross income that the Artist earns and receives. Gross income is the money that an artist receives before taxes and any expenses are deducted. This commission generally ranges from 15-to-20 percent, with 15 percent being the typical rate. It is important to be sensitive to the artist's financial position. For an example, if the artist earns $100,000 before expenses, the amount that the artist actually receives will probably be considerably less. All personnel, musicians, lawyers, accountants, etc. are paid from the artist's earnings. It is entirely possible that, after all of the bills are paid, the manager could end up making more money than the artist. As you might imagine, this would not go over very well with the artist and would certainly not contribute to a feeling of mutual trust and respect. A considerate way of handling commission with a new artist would be sharing in the artist's net earnings rather than the gross. This will endear the manager to the artist, thereby fostering trust in the manager. Once things are up and running a little more steadily, the manager can receive more money.

Many management agreements, especially those with new artists, provide for an Escalating Commission Rate, depending upon the artists monthly or yearly gross earnings. Escalating Rate Commissions are based on gross income, and is an alternative method of manager compensation. As the gross income goes up, the percentage does too. Likewise, depending on the contract, the commission rate could go down as the gross income goes up. A manager can agree to accept a flat fee from a young artist who may not be making very much money. This shows that the manager is sympathetic to the artist's position. The commission can later become a percentage. The manager should always do everything in his/her power to be fair to the artist. A manager can also agree to work for no pay at all until the artist begins to make money. The manager may then take a higher commission to make up for moneys not previously earned. The Manager collects commission on a broad range of activities and receives reimbursement from the artist for travel expenses and any other out-of-pocket expenses. Whatever is agreed to should be made clear in the management contract. Once the artist earns in excess of a certain gross amount, the manager then receives a percentage of the gross. This way, there is a more direct correlation in the earnings of the artist and manager.

Conflicts Of Interest

Conflicts of interest can be a detriment or an asset. If a Manager is involved with a booking agency, it can certainly be to the artist's benefit, just as if the manager is involved with a record company or production company. These things are all right, but it is wise for the manager to disclose this information right away. The artist should not hear this information from another source at some point down the road. It would not contribute to the feeling of mutual trust that the manager should be establishing with the artist.

Chapter 4

The Management Contract

The preliminary exploratory phase of the relationship should have unveiled many of the issues that are often so difficult to broach between an artist and manager. Issues relating to financial and legal rights and responsibilities have already been discussed. It is understandable that both parties are eager to move forward with the creative aspects of their relationship, while possibly being reluctant to sit down with attorneys to actually negotiate the management agreement. However, the management agreement is absolutely crucial to a good business relationship. Each party must clearly understand his/her rights and obligations to the other party.

Following is a list of subject areas that should be addressed:

• Manager's duties
• The artist's role
• Length of the agreement
• Manager's compensation
• Manager's expenses
• Accounting procedures
• Prior contracts still in force

Once the parties to the contract have come to a general understanding regarding what the relationship should be, each party should retain *separate legal counsel.* Each party should choose an attorney based upon that attorney's experience in the music/recording industry. It is important to retain an attorney that can anticipate the questions and issues that might come up during the term of the contract and beyond. Lawyers generally bill on an hourly basis. It is wise to ask the lawyer what his/her hourly charge is before retaining his/her services. It is also important to have some idea of how many hours the preparation and negotiation of the contract will involve.

This assures that each party has proper representation and that the terms of the contract will be clearly stated and understood. Once the contract is signed, sealed, and delivered, the parties should file the contract away and proceed as if they have a gentlemen's agreement. This keeps the relationship on friendly terms and allows the manager and artist to focus their energies on the creative aspects of the business.

See exhibit I (Management contract)

ARTIST MANAGEMENT CONTRACT

This AGREEMENT (hereinafter referred to as the "Agreement") is made effective this _____ day of _____, 200__ by and between _____, located at _____ _____ (hereinafter referred to as the "Artist") and Greta Pope Entertainment, Incorporated, located in Chicago, Illinois (hereinafter referred to as the "Manager").

WITNESSETH:

In consideration of the respective covenants contained herein, the parties hereto, intending to legally bound hereby, agree as follows:

1. Manager agrees to render advice, guidance, counsel, and other services as Artist may reasonably require to further his career as a musician, composer, actor, recording, and performing artist, and to develop new and different areas within which his artistic talents can be developed and exploited, including but not limited to the following services:

(a) to represent Artist and act as his negotiator, to fix the terms governing all manner of disposition, use, employment or exploitation of Artist's talents and the products thereof; and,

(b) to supervise Artist's professional employment, and on Artist's behalf, to consult with employers and prospective employers so as to assure the proper use and continued demand for Artist's services; and

(c) to be available at reasonable times and places to confer with Artist in connection with all matters concerning Artist's professional career, business interests, employment, and publicity; and,

(d) to exploit Artist's personality in all media, and in connection therewith, to approve and permit for the purpose of trade, advertising and publicity, the use, dissemination, reproduction or publication of Artist's name, photographic likeness, facsimile signature, voice and artistic and musical materials; and,

(e) to engage, discharge and/or direct such theatrical agents, booking agencies and employment agencies, as well as other firms, persons or corporations who may be retained for the purpose of securing contacts, engagements or employment for Artist; and,

(f) to represent Artist in all dealings with any union; and,

(g) to exercise all powers granted to Manager pursuant to Paragraph 4 hereof.

2. Manager is not required to render exclusive services to Artist or to devote his entire time or the entire time of any of Manager's employees to Artist's affairs. Nothing herein shall be construed as limiting Manager's right to represent other persons whose talents may be similar to or who may be in competition with Artist or to have and pursue business interests which may be similar to or may compete with those of Artist.

3. Artist hereby appoints Manager as his sole personal manager in all matters usually and normally within the jurisdiction and authority of personal manager, including but not limited to the advice, guidance, counsel, and direction specifically referred to in Paragraph 1 hereof. Artist agrees to seek such advice, guidance, counsel, and direction from Manager exclusively and agrees that he will not engage any other agent, representative, or manager to render similar services, and that he will not perform said services on his own behalf and he will not negotiate, accept, or execute any agreement, understanding, or undertaking concerning his career as an actor, musician, recording and performing artist without Manager's prior consent.

4. (a) Artist hereby irrevocably appoints Manager for the term of this Agreement and any extensions hereof as his true and lawful attorney-in-fact to sign, make, execute, accept, endorse, collect and deliver any and all bills of exchange, checks, and notes as his said attorney; to demand, sue for, collect, recover, and receive all goods, claims, money, interest and other items that may be due him or belong to him; and to make, execute, and deliver receipts, releases, or other discharges therefore under sale or otherwise and to defend, settle, adjust, compound, submit to arbitration and compromise all actions, suits, accounts, reckonings, claims, and demands whatsoever that are or shall be pending in such manner and in all respects as in any way limiting the foregoing; generally to do, execute and perform any other act, deed, or thing

whatsoever deemed reasonable that ought to be done, executed, and performed of any and every nature and kind as fully effectively as Artist could do if personally present; and Artist hereby ratifies and affirms all acts performed by Manager by virtue of this power of attorney.

(b) Artist expressly agrees that he will not on his own behalf exert any of the powers herein granted to Manager by the foregoing power of attorney without the express prior written consent of Manager and that all sums and considerations paid to Artist by reason of his artistic endeavors may be paid to Manager on his behalf.

(c) It is expressly understood that the foregoing power of attorney is limited to matters reasonably related to Artist's career as a musician, actor, recording and performing artist and such new and different areas within which his artistic talents can be developed and exploited.

(d) Artist agrees and understands that the power of attorney granted to Manager is coupled with an interest which Artist irrevocably grants to Manager in the career of Artist, in the artistic talents of Artist, in the products of said career and talents and in the earnings of Artist arising by reason of such career, talents, and products.

(e) Simultaneously with the execution of this Agreement, Artist shall execute a short form power-of-attorney which Manager shall be entitled to file in any jurisdiction.

5. (a) As compensation for the services to be rendered hereunder, Manager shall receive from Artist (or shall retain from Artist's net monthly earnings) at the end of each calendar month during the term hereof a sum of money equal to TEN PERCENT (10%) of Artist's net monthly income if such monthly income is less than FIVE THOUSAND ($5,000.00) dollars per month, FIFTEEN PERCENT (15%) of Artist's net monthly income if such income is more than FIVE THOUSAND ($5,000.00) dollars and less than TEN THOUSAND ($10,000) dollars per month, TWENTY PERCENT (20%) of Artist's net monthly income if such income is more than TEN THOUSAND ($10,000) dollars per month, and Artist hereby assigns to Manager an interest in such earnings to the extent of said percentages.

(b) The term "monthly gross earnings," as used herein, refers to the total of all earnings, whether in the form of salary, bonuses, royalties, interest percentages, shares of profits, merchandise, shares in ventures, products, properties, or any other kind or type of income which is reasonably related to Artist's career in the entertainment, amusement, music, recording, motion picture, television, radio, literary, theatrical, and advertising fields. The term "monthly net earnings" shall refer to the monthly gross earnings minus all costs incurred by the Manager or Artist in connection with music business operations.

(i) Royalty advances made to Artist which are deemed recoupable against future earnings by the party or parties making such royalty advances shall not be included in net monthly income.

(ii) Royalty payments made to Artist after recoupment shall be payable to Manager at the scale and rate aforementioned in Section 5a of this Agreement

(c) The compensation agreed to be paid to Manager shall be based upon net monthly earnings (as defined in Section 5b) of Artist accruing to or received by Artist during the term of this Agreement or subsequent to the termination of this agreement as a result of any services performed by Artist during the term hereof or as the result of any contract negotiated during the term hereof and any renewal, extension, or modification of this Agreement.

(d) In the event that Artist forms a corporation during the term hereof for that purpose of furnishing and exploiting his artistic talents, Artist agrees that said corporation shall offer to enter into a management contract with Manager identical in all respects to this Agreement (except as to the parties thereto). In the event that Manager accepts such offers, then the net monthly earnings of such corporation prior to the deduction of any corporate income taxes and of any corporate expenses or other deductions shall be included as a part of the Artist's net monthly earnings as herein defined, and any salary paid to Artist by such corporation shall be excluded from Artist's net monthly earnings for the purpose of calculating the compensation due to Manager hereunder.

(e) In the event that Artist forms a corporation or enters into a contract with a corporation during the term hereof for the purpose of exploiting or furnishing his artistic talents, then in addition to any and all other considerations to be paid to Manager hereunder, Manager shall be entitled to purchase at least TWENTY PERCENT (20%) of the capital stock of such corporation at the price of ONE DOLLAR ($1.00) PER SHARE. Artist agrees expressly not to enter into any contract with a corporation for such purpose unless said option is made available to Manager.

(f) Artist agrees that all net monthly earnings as herein defined may be paid directly to Manager by all persons, firms, or corporations and may not be paid by such persons, firms, or corporations to Artist, and that Manager may withhold Manager's compensation and may reimburse himself for any reasonable and receipted fees, costs, or expenses advanced or incurred by Manager that portion of Artist's gross monthly earnings which equals Manager's compensation hereunder and such disbursements incurred by Manager on behalf of Artist.

6. In the event that Manager advances any of the foregoing fees, costs, or expenses on behalf of Artist, or incurs any other reasonable expenses in connection with Artist's professional career or with the performance of Manager's services hereunder, Artist shall reimburse Manager for such fees, costs, and expenses at the end of the calendar month.

7. Artist warrants that he is under no disability, restriction, or prohibition with respect to his right to execute this Agreement and perform its terms and conditions. Artist further warrants and represents that no act or omission by Artist hereunder will violate any right or liability to any person. Artist agrees to indemnify Manager and hold Manager harmless against any damages, costs, expenses, fees (including attorney's fees) incurred by Manager in any claim, suit, litigation, or proceeding instituted against Manager and arising out of any breach or claimed breach by Artist of any warranty, representation, or covenant of Artist. Artist agrees to exert his best reasonable efforts to further his promotional career during the term of this Agreement, and to cooperate with Manager to the fullest extent in the interest of promoting Artist's career.

8. The initial term of this Agreement shall be for a period of TWO (2) YEARS.

9. Manager agrees to maintain accurate books and records of all transactions concerning Artist. In the event of an audit, books and records may be inspected during regular business hours by a Certified Public Accountant designated by Artist upon 30 days notice to Manager.

10. During the term of this Agreement, it is understood and agreed that

there shall be no change or modification of this Agreement unless reduced to writing and signed by all parties hereto. No waiver or any breach of this Agreement shall be construed as a continuing waiver or consent to any subsequent breach hereof.

11. It is agreed that as a condition precedent to any assertion by Artist or Manager that the other is in default in performing any obligation contained herein, the party alleging the default must advise the other in writing by Certified United States Mail of the specific obligation which it claims has been breached and said other party shall be allowed a period of SIXTY (60) days from the receipt of such written notice within which to cure such default.

12. This Agreement does not and shall not be construed to create a partnership or joint venture between the parties hereto.

13. This Agreement shall be construed in accordance with the laws of the State of _____STATE_____ governing contracts executed and performed therein, and shall be binding upon and inure to the benefit of the parties, respective heirs, executors, administrators, successors, and assigns.

IN WITNESS WHEREOF, the parties hereto have executed this Agreement on the day and year first above written.

AGREED TO AND ACCEPTED:

BY:
"ARTIST"
<<FULL NAME>>

_____
 (an authorized signatory)

BY:
"MANAGER"
Greta Pope Entertainment, Incorporated

_____
 (an authorized signatory)

[End of contract]

Chapter 5

Managing the Artist

One of the most important decisions that an artist is faced with is whether or not to engage a Personal Manager. If the artist chooses to work with a personal manager, that manager becomes the single most important person in the artist's professional life. A good personal manager can expand an artist's career to its maximum potential, while a bad one can rocket the artist into absolute oblivion.

What exactly is the Manager's job? What should the artist expect from a manager?

A Personal Manager provides advice and direction to the development of the artist's career. A manager is the artist's personal representative. He/she is a planner, advisor, organizer, strategist, overseer, manipulator, coordinator, detail person, traveling companion, and friend. The manager's job is to follow through on anything and everything that will further the artist's career. The manager is the only other person, besides the artist, that is involved with all aspects of the artist's career. One way to view the artist/manager relationship is that the artist is the Corporation and the manager is the CEO of that corporation. A manager should be honest with the artist and encourage the artist to also be honest with him/her, with regard to what the artist's needs and interests might be.

There are several ways that the Manager/Artist relationship can work.

Does the artist need and/or want total management or is a limited management relationship more comfortable and appropriate?

Total Management -- The Manager handles every aspect of the artist's career including interacting with musicians, lawyers, accountants, marketing people, venue owners, and others. The duties also include developing the artist's image, performance material, marketing materials, etc.

Limited Management -- Manager handles only the things that the artist requests. For example, the artist may wish to hire and interact with his/her own accountant and lawyers or the artist may want to work directly with the musicians. So the Manager would not handle those things. This is often the case with an artist who is just starting out when there is not enough money generated to warrant the manager's involvement in every aspect of the business. Once the artist becomes busy, the Manager generally takes over these duties.

The manager must always strive to create a feeling of trust within the artist/manager relationship. If handled properly, this relationship can and should last for many years, culminating in real friendship and high regard between the artist and manager.

A Manager is not expected, nor is he/she required to provide, any financial assistance to the artist. A Manager is not a booking agent and, by law, is not authorized to procure employment on the artist's behalf unless he or she has an agent's license. If the manager does not have an agent's license he/she must secure an agent to find work for the artist. The things that the manager may do for the artist are:

Locate and contract with venues for showcases where the artist can perform to gain experience and begin to develop a following. This is the first step on the road to success. It is important that the venue be appropriate for the artist. Will the artist's following be comfortable coming to see the artist at the venue? An upscale audience with fancy vehicles might not be comfortable going to a venue in a questionable area with no secure parking. It is important to consider "Who is this artist's following?" and "Who would we like the artist's following to be?" "Who are we trying to attract?" "Where would they be willing to come to see this artist?"

The manager selects musicians, along with the road manager, staff and tech crew. He or she, along with the artist, also selects the material to be performed. Locating rehearsal space and scheduling rehearsals is also a part of the manager's job. The Manager handles all aspects of preparing for the performance.

The manager plans and publicizes the artist's performances and showcases, as well as identifies and negotiates the contract or agreement with the performance venue. The contract is usually a simple document that states the following things:

- parties to the contract (manager, artist, venue, and venue representative)
- location of performance
- general description of performance
- duration of performance
- fee to be paid to artist
- when the fee is due
- is a deposit due with contract signature? When is balance due?
- date of the performance
- time of the performance
- number of performers/description of performers
- statement regarding merchandise sales
- does the venue take a percentage of revenue from sales?
- location of merchandise sales stations
- number of merchandise stations to be made available to artist

Successful artists will often have a contract rider, which provides more detail than the contract. The contract rider should include any special requests made by the artist, such as adequate dressing room space or meals to be provided. It can also include equipment needs and load-in information. Signatures from the artist and/or artist representative (manager) and the venue representative make the contract and the contract rider legally binding. The signatures indicate that all parties agree to comply with the conditions set forth in the contract and rider. These agreements serve as guidelines, ensuring a smooth experience for everyone involved. After locating and contracting with the venue, the manager then proceeds with marketing the performance showcase.

New Trends

A new trend in artist management is to offer artists and their fans Internet exposure never before seen in traditional artist/manager relationships. Some management companies have been able to tie their artists into major corporate websites, giving great exposure to their clients. These websites allow fans to interact with the artists via email. The corporations benefit because the artist's fans are drawn to the websites and as a result, learn more about the products and services of the corporation. This practice also allows the manager to benefit from having fan email addresses for target marketing purposes. An effective example of this tactic is singer Celine Dion's association with Coty fragrances. There are three scents associated with Celine Dion:

Celine Dion Parfums
Celine Dion Chic
Celine Dion Sensational

Visit www.celinedionbeauty.com to see how this works. The website gives viewers lots of information, including a store locator to find the Coty fragrance products. There is also an opportunity to sign up for an e-mail list that benefits the Coty Fragrance Company as well as the Celine Dion organization. Also included on this website is a link to Celine Dion's personal artist website. It's a win-win situation for everyone involved.

Artist Website

In this modern era, it is crucial that the artist have a business website. It is very common for potential clients, agents, promoters, etc. to visit the artist's website for information. It is the manager's job to identify a good webmaster and oversee the building of a comprehensive website for the artist, where fans can find basic biographical information, access the artist's schedule of performances, hear audio clips, see photos, and view videos. This website should offer fans a means of communicating with the artist and allow fans to become a part of the artist's mailing list.

The artist's website should function as a business center where fans, agents, event planners, perspective bookers, and media/press can get complete information about the artist. Having an engaging and comprehensive website saves time for the artist and the manager. When the artist is contacted through the website, the inquirer already has a great deal of information and is very possibly ready to book the artist.

A website requires action on the part of the inquirer, in that they must make an effort to go to the artist's website. For this reason, it is also good to put into place a means of reaching out to fans or to people that represent work for the artist. There are several email communication software tools that allow the artist or manager to trigger a response from a given group. The recipient has only to click on a provided link to be directed to the artist's website or to see whatever the manager/artist wants them to see. This communication tool can provide a link to video, audio, press releases or absolutely anything. This type of communication allows the manager/artist to further build the artist's brand by presenting materials and information in a very direct way. For example, if the artist is looking to book four dates in St. Louis for the month of October, the artist or manager can identify venues in that area, prepare an email blast and send communication to 50 venues in the area. From those 50 venues, the artist is very likely to realize the four desired bookings. This communication also puts the artist on the radar screen of the contacted venues for possible future bookings.

Email communication is good for keeping fans abreast of the artist's performances, activities and accomplishments. This helps fans feel close to the artist and allows them to offer maximum support to the artist through attending performances, buying merchandise, and spreading the word about the artist.

There are several user-friendly, web-based email communication services such as iContact and Constant Contact that make it easy to send large numbers of email notices in one click. There is a fee for these services, but it is a worthwhile investment and can send a professional looking email to thousands of people at once. The success of this type of service is again contingent upon getting email addresses at each performance and taking the time to enter the data gathered after each performance. Also these services provide a code where fans can join the artists' mailing list directly from his/her website.

Social Networking

The manager can also use internet social networking sites as valuable tools in gaining exposure for their artist. A few such sites are myspace, twitter, LinkedIn and facebook. These sites allow fans to keep abreast of the artist's activities, tours, philanthropy, and other things that might be of interest. Links from these social networking sites to the artist's own website should also be in place.

Social networking is an important and effective means of garnering fans and bringing attention to the artist. Creating a facebook fan page for the artist on www.facebook.com will allow the manager to "tell the artist's story." After a little practice, you'll find that facebook is very user friendly. A facebook fan page is an on-going way for fans to learn about the artist. The feature photo and information can be changed, but the page is something that would permanently remain in place. It also allows the manager to communicate easily with the people that become fans of the artist through that vehicle. Information can be included on the fan page to direct people to the artist's website or to other websites that might have additional information or press about the artist.

The artist's facebook fans can be put into lists based upon interest or geographical location. This will allow for target marketing of fans interested in particular offerings that the artist might have. Geographical location lists are very helpful for notifying fans of a touring artist's concert in their city. Facebook also allows the manager to create an Event Page to advertise a specific event or showcase that the artist might be doing. A new event page would be created for every event or showcase that the artist does. Fans and friends can be individually invited and can respond by indicating "yes" they will attend, "maybe" they will attend or "no" they will not attend. There is also a field where invitees can make comments, send good wishes and more.

The Facebook Event Page can also be set up so that only the administrator (the person that created the page) can see who is attending the event and who is not. This is sometimes desirable, particularly if there is concern that the attendance numbers will be small. The manager always wants to present a positive image for the Artist.

There are other social networking sites that work similarly. Among them are myspace, twitter and LinkedIn. Myspace (www.myspace.com) is a good site for advertising the artist's events. Twitter (www.twitter.com) is a great way to frequently send short "headlines" regarding the artist's activities, concerts, rehearsals, merchandise or other things that might be of interest to fans. There is also LinkedIn (www.linkedin.com) which is a site for business professionals.

Success in using social networking sites is dependent upon taking the time to build contacts on the sites. Communication can only be made with people that are in the artist's network and are among the artist's contacts. Therefore, it is important to make as many contacts as possible.

Often Public Relations Firms (P.R.) will create social network client pages and build contacts for their clients. P.R. companies will "tweet" (www.twitter. com) and completely manage social networking for their clients. However, at the beginning of an artist's career, there probably will not be money to retain a P.R. Firm to perform those tasks. It will most likely be the responsibility of the artist or the manager to handle all social networking tasks. Social networking is important and should be taken seriously as the manager and artist work together to "brand" and build name recognition.

In addition to Social Networking, other types of marketing and advertising must be in place to ensure a good turn-out for the artist's showcase. Two months before the showcase, the Manager should design, create and produce flyers, postcards, posters, and email blasts publicizing the artist's showcase. Utilizing the appropriate software, these marketing materials can be easily created on the Manager's computer. For large-scale printing, it is best to email the marketing pieces to an office support center like Fed-Ex Kinko's, Staples, or Office Max for fast, high-quality and relatively inexpensive printing.

The Manager then goes about the business of distributing those materials to places that will produce the biggest impact. Materials should be placed everywhere that the artist frequents, including the artist's hair salon/barber shop, grocery store, church, gym--anyplace where the artist is known. The materials should also be placed at the Manager's grocery store, hair salon/

barber shop, etc. The Manager's name or company name should be mentioned on the marketing materials because the Manager might have contacts that recognize his/her name. Marketing materials should be placed in all businesses, etc. near the venue so that people that spend time in the neighborhood are aware of the performance. Since they're already in the area, they may come to the performance.

The Manager should place a "fan list" sheet in a prominent location at each performance and ask audience members for their contact information such as email addresses. Audience members should be assured that their info will only be used to advise them of upcoming performances of the artist. This will begin to develop a mailing list. This sheet should ask for the audience member's name, mailing address and email address. This way, the Manager can begin to send out postcards and emails for upcoming performances. This creates a following.

Fan list sample: *See exhibit 2*

Exhibit 2

Greta Pope Entertainment, Inc. provides entertainment for all types of public and private events throughout the area. We'd like to keep you posted on our upcoming activities. Please print clearly.

Name   Email   Address

1._____

2._____

3._____

4._____

5._____

6._____

7._____

8._____

9._____

10._____

11._____

12._____

13._____

Once all of the marketing and preparations for the performance have been completed, the manager has additional duties that take place during or immediately following the performance. When the advertising work is finished and the manager has secured a robust audience for the showcase, the manager's attention turns to making sure that the venue is ready for the artist's showcase.

The Manager communicates with the venue about comforts for the artist, including green room availability, food and drinks, equipment load-in, equipment case storage area for the band, artist and band dressing rooms and other things that have been agreed to in the contract and rider. Stage set-up and sound/lighting check should be scheduled several hours before the showcase begins. The Manager should present a sound and lighting chart to the venue tech people for execution during the showcase. The Manager might also place programs or postcards on the tables or on chairs, featuring the artist's biography and the manager's contact information, along with the artist's website and social networking sites. If the artist has merchandise available, the Manager would arrange with the venue to have it displayed for sale in a prominent spot. The programs placed on the tables might also list the location of the merchandise sale kiosk, the items available, and the pricing. The Manager should make arrangements for audio and video recording for the showcase. These materials can be used for marketing the artist for future performances.

Once the showcase is underway, the Manager should observe the performance and the artist's impact on the audience. The Manager then begins to clearly define and create the artist's image. Everything from the music that the artist performs, to the script or patter that the artist uses to communicate with the audience, to the artist's appearance and wardrobe. Everything affects the audience's perception of the artist.

Before or after the Showcase, the manager might also talk with audience members to get a sense of their perception of the artist. The Manager might ask:

How did you like the performance?
Do you live nearby?
What brought you out to this performance?

Do you know the artist?

Are you a fan of this type of music?

Do you go to concerts often?

...and other questions that might help the manager better understand the artist's audience.

The Manager might also use this opportunity to get contact information from audience members for future use in email campaigns or postcard mailings.

Generate press interest in the artist

The manager should spend time leading up to the concert creating a press list. This list should include contacts for:

- Local and Regional Newspapers
- Feature story if possible
- Community Events section
- Trade Magazines
- Feature Story if possible
- Local events section
- Television
- Community Calendars
- Interviews
- Radio
- Community Calendars
- Interviews
- Play the artist's music on-air
- Venue Marketing

Include artist's name and performance date in all of the venue's communication to their following, including venue's snail mail announcements, email announcements and website postings, etc.,

invite recording executives, club owners, corporate event planners, etc. to the showcases.

Once the artist has begun to get his/her feet wet in the business, the personal manager's duties expand. Some of the most important aspects of the manager's job become:

- Helping the artist with major business decisions, such as deciding which recording company to sign with, whether to make a publishing deal, what the artist fee structure should be, etc.
- Assisting with the artist's creative process, such as selecting material for live performance and recording, selecting a producer, selecting and hiring band members, etc.
- Promoting the artists career by talking the artist up with everyone that he or she meets and coordinating a publicity campaign, etc.
- Organizing, heading up and overseeing the artist's professional team of lawyers, business managers, and agents.
- Working with agents and promoters in coordinating concert tours and hiring all personnel for the tours
- Pushing the record company to make sure that the artist's recordings are treated as priorities
- Being a general buffer between the artist and the outside world and keeping the artist's name before the public to build and maintain brand recognition

The Manager becomes responsible for promotion, publicity, and the general necessities of running the artist's business. He or she will find an agent to handle the artist's bookings as well as assembling a support team of lawyers, accountants, road managers, and business managers. A Personal Manager does not always travel with the artists that they represent. Instead, a tour manager or road manager is engaged at the artist's expense. This person handles the artist's business on the road, such as transportation, hotels, fee collections, as well as stage, sound, and lighting needs. The road manager also serves as a buffer for the artist from fans, charitable organizations, endorsements, and appearances. Their duties also include merchandise display, inventory control, managing revenue from sales, and many other things. Depending upon the popularity of the Artist, the size of the venue, the production size, and the demand for the Artist's merchandise, the tour or road manager might have a small, medium sized or large staff to handle all of the necessary tasks related to a smooth operation. The tour or road manager works under the personal manager and acts on his/her behalf while the artist is on the road. This allows the personal manager the freedom to continue marketing the artist, branding the artist, and keeping the artist's image before the public in the interest of securing future engagements and endorsements.

The Personal Manager must also see that the artist's credibility remains intact. The manager must consider the impact of each commercial deal, product endorsement, interview, and public appearance. The long-range effect of endorsements, commercials, interviews and public appearances must elevate the artist's profile in a positive way, while providing immediate financial gain and potential for future financial gain. Credibility is very important to the artist. The public must like the artist and believe in the artist in order for that artist to have any kind of longevity. A Manager must always have the artist's best interest at heart, because after all, success for the artist means success for the Manager. A Manager's good taste and judgment is as important as any other asset that he or she may possess.

The Manager must have a keen sense of market positioning and a clear concept of the artist's assets. The Manager must develop a strategy for fully exploiting the artist's assets as well as developing a strategy for marketing the artist to the segment of the population that will be most receptive. The Manager should work closely with the artist, discussing all major decisions so that each of them is happy with the image that is portrayed and the approach that will be taken to reach the mutually desired goal. The manager/artist relationship will hopefully be a long and fruitful one. It is wise that the Manager move slowly and very deliberately with the artist, making sure that there is a clear meeting of the minds with regard to all major decisions. This will avoid confusion down the road..

The Manager is responsible for day-to-day career development, personal advice, guidance and planning the long-range direction of the artist's career. It has been said about successful manager/artist relationships, that the artist is a mere figment of his or her manager's imagination.

Chapter 6

Agents

The personal manager is at the helm of the artist's business, handling all personnel and activities pertinent to the artist's success. Let's take a closer look at other personnel necessary to the artist's organization.

Agents

The role of an agent in the music business is an important one. An agent is the "broker" that connects the artist to the job. The agent is responsible for booking the artist for live personal appearances and concerts. Agents are also often involved with connecting the artist with commercials, tour sponsorship, television specials, etc. Agents do not get involved with, nor are they paid for recordings or songwriting.

Agents are regulated by the following unions:

AFM: American Federation of Musicians

The American Federation of Musicians of the United States and Canada is the largest organization in the world representing the interests of professional musicians. Whether negotiating fair agreements, protecting ownership of recorded music, securing benefits such as health care and pension, or lobbying our legislators, the AFM is committed to raising industry standards and placing the professional musician in the foreground of the cultural landscape. www. afm.org

AFTRA: American Federation of Television and Radio Artists

The American Federation of Television and Radio Artists (AFTRA) is a national labor union representing over 70,000 performers, journalists and other artists working in the entertainment and news media. AFTRA's scope of representation covers: broadcast, public and cable television (news, sports and weather; drama and comedy, soaps, talk and variety shows, documentaries, children's programming, reality and game shows); radio (news, commercials, hosted programs); sound recordings (CDs, singles, Broadway cast albums, audio books); "non-broadcast," and industrial material as well as Internet and digital programming. AFTRA's membership includes an array of talentósound recording membership includes artists who bring pop, rock, country, classical, folk, jazz, comedy, Latin, hip hop, rap and R&B to the world. AFTRA members perform in television and radio advertising, non-broadcast video, audio books and messaging, and provide their skills for developing technologies such as interactive games and Internet material. (www.aftra.org)

SAG: Screen Actor's Guild

Screen Actors Guild is the nation's largest labor union representing working actors. Established in 1933, SAG has a rich history in the American labor movement, from standing up to studios to break long-term engagement contracts in the 1940s; to fighting for artists' rights amid the digital revolution sweeping the entertainment industry in the 21st Century. With 20 branches nationwide, SAG represents nearly 120,000 working actors in film, television, industrials, commercials, video games, music videos and other new media. The Guild exists to enhance actors' working conditions, compensation and benefits and to be a powerful, unified voice on behalf of artists' rights. Headquartered in Los Angeles, SAG is a proud affiliate of the AFL-CIO. (www.sag.org)

AEA: Actor's Equity Association

Actors' Equity Association ("AEA" or "Equity"), founded in 1913, is the labor union that represents more than 45,000 Actors and Stage Managers in the United States. Equity seeks to advance, promote and foster the art of live theatre as an essential component of our society. Equity negotiates wages and working conditions and provides a wide range of benefits, including health and pension plans, for its members. Actors' Equity is a member of the AFL-CIO, and is affiliated with FIA, an international organization of performing arts unions. (www.actorsequity.org)

The unions put a cap on the commission rate for agents. That commission rate is 10%. There is sometimes a place for the artist to initial on the agent/artist contract giving the agent a commission of the artist's earnings from recordings. The manager should make sure that the artist *does not* agree to this. The agent is not entitled to *any* commission from recordings.

The union regulating of agents is called franchising. The unions only allow their members to be represented by "franchised" agents. The franchised agent only uses contracts approved by the union. This protects the artist from possible abuses.

Agents will often work on a sliding commission scale, so that as the artist's earnings go up, the commission rate goes down.

The major thing to negotiate for the artist is the term of the contract with the agent. Most agents want a contract with a term of three years or more. This is a long time if things are not working out. Negotiate for a one-year contract instead and include the need for minimum levels of income as part of the contract. This assures that the agent must secure enough work to provide the artist with a certain level of income within a certain time period, or the artist can terminate the contract. If things are going well, great, if not, you can find the artist a new agent.

It is beneficial for the manager to use the services of agents booking the types of jobs that meet the artist's interest. For example, if the artist wants cruise line work, college tours, or corporate work, be sure to work with agents that specialize in those areas. It's also beneficial to enlist agents in the geographical area where the artist hopes to work. For example, if the artist will be working in Europe, you should engage an agent that has knowledge of European venues and opportunities. This will assure that the artist's time and talents are put to the highest and best use. Many large American agencies use local sub-agents for foreign territories.

Choosing an agent is the job of the manager since the manager will be the point person. It is important to work with an agent with whom you can easily get along.

Chapter 7

Attorneys

The role of attorneys in the music business is to structure deals and shape the artist's business life. Attorneys have become very powerful in this arena because they are involved in all areas of the business and, because of the short duration of time that they have to spend with each client, they're able to be involved in many deals. This keeps them on the cutting edge of the business. They can be influential in determining which company gets the deal, so the companies want to keep them happy. They can also influence other segments of the business, such as which business managers or personal managers get a particular client. As a result of this, the business and personal managers want to keep the lawyers happy as well. All of these things make the attorneys very powerful.

In searching for a lawyer for your client, make sure that the individual is competent in the field. There are many types of lawyers specializing in all areas of the legal profession. There are real estate attorneys, tax attorneys, criminal attorneys, etc. Make sure that you are dealing with an attorney who specializes in the *music business* and *entertainment law*. This is very important. Just because an individual is a lawyer doesn't mean that he or she is the best choice for your client. Do your homework and be informed.

Find out what kinds of relationships the lawyer has in the business. If a lawyer is highly regarded in his field, record companies and other major players will treat them well and respond to their requests because lawyers provide business for the record companies, managers, and others. A lawyer with good relationships will get your deal done quicker and more effectively.

Compensation

Lawyers charge clients in a variety of ways. Some charge an hourly rate, ranging from approximately $150-$600 per hour. Some charge a percentage of the artist's revenue (usually about 5%). Others charge in a way that is known as *value billing* often with an hourly rate or *retainer* against it. A retainer is a set monthly fee, which can be either credited against the ultimate fee or it can be a flat fee covering all of the services that the attorney is performing for your client. With value billing, the lawyer asks for a fee upon completion of the deal. This fee is based upon the size of the deal and the attorney's contribution to its fruition. It's a good idea to be clear on how the billing is determined *before* becoming involved with an attorney. This allows you and your client to be prepared to pay the attorney.

Conflict Of Interest

A conflict of interest occurs when an attorney is representing clients on both sides of the deal. For example, an attorney might represent your client and the record company, for example. The interests of these two parties are adverse and should cause you concern. If you find yourself in this situation, you would be wise to secure another attorney's service. Your client's attorney should always have your client's best interest at heart to the exclusion of any other party to the deal.

When interviewing an attorney, you should ask if they foresee any conflicts of interest. This will avoid potential problems down the road. There are also some other things that you'll want to know about a potential legal representative for your client before signing an agreement:

Duration of the agreement
Conditions for termination
Fees
Are costs separate, i.e. photocopying, faxing, etc.
References from mangers, artists, etc., at your level of success

Chapter 8

Business Managers

Though some personal managers undertake the task of financial guidance and investment advice for their artists, most successful artists opt to engage a *Business Manager* for this job. The business manager is usually an accountant or tax attorney. The business manager usually collects the artist's earnings, pays the manager and other people working for the artist, manages the artist's investments, and is mindful of tax consequences for the artist. The business manager generally receives 2-to-6 percent of the artist's gross earnings, however sometimes an annual or monthly flat fee is agreed upon. The business manager should have some degree of expertise in the areas of sales, marketing, public relations, data processing, operations, budgeting, accounting, finance, statistics, economics, and tax auditing. In today's world, a business manager should also have a working knowledge of frequently used computer software programs.

Marketing

In this segment, we'll talk a little about marketing, as marketing is crucial to the success of any artist. Marketing is the key to success for any business. Determine what demographic or segment of the population is the artist's potential following. Does the artist appeal to screaming teen-aged girls, or urban thirty-somethings, or a fundamentalist Christian audience, or possibly a mature senior audience? Once a basic idea of the artist's target demographic is determined, a marketing plan can be put into place.

Marketing is an ongoing integrated process that promotes a good or service. Marketing is used to cultivate the customer, satisfy the customer and build a strong relationship with the customer in order to realize value from that customer down the road. In this time of fierce competition in the marketplace, it is not enough to have a good product. Anticipating the customer's needs and satisfying them more effectively than your competitors is crucial.

Marketing is the process of building "brand" so that the consumer begins to have faith in the artist's product. For an example, you want the artist's fans know that they will enjoy the music that the artist presents and that the volume and song selection will be to their liking. Equally they will come to know that the artist will always perform at venues that they will enjoy and that the artist always takes into consideration, when selecting a venue, that secure parking will be available. Things of this nature can contribute to or detract from the brand.

One of the greatest brands in the world is McDonald's. When you go to a McDonald's restaurant, you know exactly what to expect. No matter where you are in the world, the brand is recognizable and consistent. This is what the manager should try to achieve for the artist. Be consistent with the image. *Those that like who you are and what you do will gravitate to you.*

Marketing is described by the American Marketing Association as "the activity, set of institutions, and processes for creating, delivering, and exchanging offerings that have value for customers, clients, partners, and society at large." (www.marketingpower.com) The Chartered Institute of Marketing defines marketing as "the management process responsible for identifying, anticipating and satisfying customer requirements profitably." Value Based Marketing defines marketing as "the management process that seeks to maximize returns to shareholders by developing relationships with valued customers and creating a competitive advantage.

So as you can see, marketing is not so much about the product as it is about building a strong and trusted relationship with the customer. In the past, marketing was viewed as a creative industry, but due to new research that shows that today's highly effective marketing strategies make use of the social sciences, mathematics, psychology, sociology, economics and so on, marketing is now considered a science. (www.wikipedia.org)

Advertising

Advertising works hand-in-hand with marketing. Advertising as defined by Merriam-Webster is "the action of calling something to the attention of the public especially by paid announcements. It is the business of preparing advertisements for publication or broadcast." (www.merriam-webster.com)

The manager might pay to advertise a particular show or group of shows that the artist is doing. This can be done via newspapers, magazines, postcards, flyers, email blasts, blogs, word-of-mouth, billboards, public appearances, and other means.

Public Relations (P.R.)

The third spoke in the wheel is Public Relations. Public Relations is the practice of managing the communication between an organization and its public. Public Relations gives the artist exposure to the public through credible third party outlets including newspapers, magazines, radio, television, etc. These third party outlets give the artist legitimacy that advertising does not. Public relations might involve the scheduling of radio or television interviews, feature articles in newspapers or magazines, participation in parades or other public appearances

Engaging a professional Marketing, Advertising and P.R. firm is instrumental in building a brand and getting that brand before the public. The manager should take on the responsibility of identifying the marketing, advertising and P.R. firms, as he or she will interface with these entities as the primary point person.

Musicians

Musicians are an integral part of any recording or live performance. The number of musicians will vary depending upon the size of the act and the style of music being performed. Musicians must be well rehearsed, well trained, experienced, and disciplined. Always get the best quality musicians that you can afford. On a tour where the group is performing night after night, musicians must be able to keep up with the rigors of the schedule. They must know how to pace themselves and be fresh for each performance.

Trained, experienced, professional musicians will make your work easy. They have impeccable technique on their instruments, they are able to read music charts, they are capable of playing many styles of music and they bring professional expertise to the table that will invariably improve your project. There is always a great benefit to hiring professional musicians.

Music arrangements are written, usually by a musical director, who will also be a member of the band. This individual is the first musician hired by the manager. The musical director handles all things related to the music and musicians. He or she will write arrangements, rehearse the band, lead the band, make sure that musicians arrive on time, and that they are ready to play at the designated times. The musical director meets with the manager and the artist to get a clear understanding of what songs will be performed and how the arrangements should be written.

In groups where music charts are used, whether for recording or for live appearances, the musical director is responsible for putting the charts on each musician's music stand before the performance and collecting and organizing them at the end of the performance. He or she is responsible for storing the charts and making sure that they are transported from one performance location to the next. In the case of an orchestra or other large performing group, a music librarian would be employed to keep the music organized and easily accessible. He or she works closely with the musical director to ensure that everything runs smoothly.

Chapter 9

Recording
Major Label vs. Independent Label

Major Labels

Once the artist has signed a record deal with a major recording label, the Manager's job expands yet again. He or she then becomes responsible for interfacing with the recording company personnel including A&R (Artists and Repertoire). A&R is the department of a record company responsible for signing and providing creative assistance to new artists. The following information about the recording industry has been taken directly from the online website Wikipedia.

"There are many benefits to signing with a major label. Composers and performers get part of their income from writers' copyright collectives and performance rights organizations such as the ASCAP (American Society of Composers, Authors and Publishers) and BMI (Broadcast Music Incorporated). These societies and collectives ensure that composers and performers are compensated when their works are used on the radio or TV or in films. When musicians and singers make a CD or DVD, the creative process is often coordinated by a record producer, whose role in the recording may range from suggesting songs and backing musicians to having a direct hands-on role in the studio, coaching singers, giving advice to session musicians on playing styles, and working with the senior sound engineer to shape the recorded sound through effects and mixing. Some professional musicians, bands, and singers sign with record labels, which are companies that finance the recording process in return for part or full share of the rights to the recording.

Record label companies manage brands and trademarks in the course of marketing the recordings, and they can also oversee the production of videos for broadcast or retail sale. Labels may comprise a *record group* of one or more label companies, plus ancillary businesses such as manufacturers and distributors. A record group may be, in turn, part of a *music group* which includes music publishers. Publishers represent the rights in the compositions, the music as written, rather than as recorded, and are traditionally separate entities from the record label companies. The publisher of the composition for each recording may or may not be part of the record label's music group; many publishers are wholly independent and are owned by the artists themselves."

The four major recording labels as of this writing are:

Universal Music Group
Sony Music Entertainment
Warner Music Group
EMI Group

In the 21st Century, many artists are producing their own recording projects on Independent or "indie" labels. Some artists are writing and recording original material while others are recording well known songs written by other songwriters. It's important when recording music written by others, to pay royalties to that artist. ASCAP (The American Society of Composers, Authors and Publishers) www.ascap.com and BMI (Broadcast Music, Inc.) www.bmi.com are both able to assist with procuring licensing for copyrighted and published music. The Harry Fox Agency can also offer help in this area. For more information on the Harry Fox Agency, visit www.harryfox.com.

"Indie" Labels

Artists recording on small "indie" labels do not have the benefit of the many support services that the major labels can offer. One of the most important of those support services is marketing and distribution. Producing a recording project, while challenging, is the easy part. Selecting material, contracting with musicians, along with choosing a recording studio, and a great engineer are the creative aspects of doing a recording project. Many artists have taken on this challenge and have created very good, professional quality products.

Unfortunately, several years, or in some cases, several decades after completing the recording, many of these artists find themselves with large quantities of CDs in their garages or basements. Making the public aware of the recording is the difficult task. This is where the major label marketing and distribution capabilities really make a difference with getting the artist exposure and selling their CDs. However with a little research, planning and hard work the "indie" artist can find success with CD sales. CDs can be sold at live performances and on the artist's website. Songs can also be placed for sale on i-tunes and other such sites, where they can be made available to the entire world. I am aware of a young acoustic pop band called *Every Wakes Dream*. These guys have recorded an E.P. ("extended play") CD entitled *Becoming the Wave* that is currently available on i-tunes. They are having tremendous success selling their EP at their concerts as well as selling individual songs to their fans around the world via the internet. Granted, these guys are young and their following is also young and very web savvy, but any independent label artist can do well by selling CDs and other merchandise in this way. It is also important that the artist and his/her manager keep abreast of new technological developments available to boost CD and merchandise sales via the internet. Additionally, when the artist puts the work out him/herself, they may gain the attention of a major label who will come courting.

Recording the Indie Project

The term "Indie" simply means an independent recording project that is not produced or funded by a major recording label. Many artists are recording in this manner today and often finding good sales success with their projects. Relatively inexpensive digital recording equipment has made it possible for a person to, in the privacy of their own home, create a quality recording project. Many artists are writing their own material, recording and distributing it. Before the advent of the internet, successful Indie projects were virtually unheard of. The Internet has allowed artists to market and distribute their recording projects, while building a large fan base, all without the benefit of the major label recording companies.

The first step in recording your own "Indie" product is to select the material that you wish to record. Some artists prefer to record cover tunes, while others write or acquire original songs for their recordings. Then there are artists that use a combination of both.

When an artist records a song written by someone else, that artist will owe royalties to the writer of the song, as the song is the intellectual property of the songwriter. When an artist writes his/her own songs, they can use the recorded music in any way that they want. As an example, I host and produce a radio show for which I use several of my original songs for theme music. It is my right to use my intellectual property as I wish. To protect your intellectual property, be sure to copyright your original material. (www.copyright.gov)

Once the material has been selected, the artist would then identify musicians to play on the project. The artist and manager work closely with the musical director to create and develop musical arrangements for all of the songs. Once the arrangements are complete to everyone's satisfaction, the search for musicians begins. It will be clear what instruments are needed through the arrangements that have been prepared. The musical director is a good source for identifying musicians. The selected musicians should be of the highest quality that the artist can afford, but they should also be individuals that the musical director likes, respects and can get along with. Having a congenial group of musicians will keep problems to a minimum during the recording sessions and throughout your working time together.

The next steps are rehearsing the band and locating a good recording studio. Rehearsing the band might require that you borrow or rent a space where all the musicians can comfortably fit and where the music will not disturb neighbors. There are warehouses or actual rehearsal spaces available for rent in most cities. Some clubs will allow bands to rehearse on their premises during the daytime. When the band is rehearsed to perfection, you're ready to go into the studio and record your project.

Finding the right recording studio is very important. Recording time in a professional studio can be expensive, however it is always best to go to a high quality, professional studio. I know of an artist who wanted to save money on his recording. He decided to use a studio in a "guy's basement" that would cost him half of what the high quality professional studio was charging. I advised the artist against this because a good engineer in a professional studio will save you time, thereby controlling your cost and maximizing your quality. During the recording sessions, the "guy in the basement" needed to make a phone call every hour or so to his "mentor" to help him understand how to use his own equipment.

This was eating into the artist's paid time. The fact was, the guy really didn't know what he was doing. I later found out that the guy's "mentor" was the engineer at the high quality professional studio that I had originally suggested that the artist use. In the final analysis, the artist ended up paying more than he would have paid had he used the professional studio. Though the "guy in the basement" charged half of the hourly rate that the professional studio would have charged, it took him more than twice as long to produce a mediocre recording. As it turned out, the artist paid more money for an inferior product. Don't let this heartbreaking scenario happen to you.

A professional is a professional and will invariably do a better job. This is true for recording engineers, musicians, singers, managers and anyone else that you will encounter in this business. The price may be higher for their service, but this is for good reason. A professional is able to expedite the job as a result of extensive training and experience. Don't waste your money or your time with anyone else.

After you have recorded, mixed and mastered your CD, you'll need to consider CD cover artwork. Your cover will be very important in marketing and selling your CD. It should be compelling and expressive of the type of music that you've recorded. It should also be expressive of you as an artist. A good graphic designer can help you with this. Photos or any type of image can be used for your cover. You can also use text only. A creative graphic designer will present you with several options from which to choose. In addition to the cover, you'll want the designer to create the entire insert for the CD. The insert can consist of 2-panels (one page front and back) or you can have any number of panels that you want. I have seen projects with up to 8-panels or more. Some inserts are folded and some are designed as small booklets. You'll also want the graphic artist to create a tray design for the CD case. This design will be under the CD as it sits in the CD case. It is up to you and the artist to determine how the package will be put together.

The insert should have the title of your CD on the front panel, along with any artwork that you've chosen. The insert should also list the songs on the CD in addition to the songwriter and duration of the song. All musicians, engineers, mixing engineers, producers, and anyone involved with the project should be credited on the insert. Some artists feature the lyrics of the songs, some don't. A dedication or special "thank you" might also be included. Every project is different and it is up to the artist to determine the overall look and content of the CD.

You will want to include a bar code with the CD title, pricing, and other pertinent information encoded. You'll also want to have each CD shrink wrapped. This is where a good recording studio or an online packaging company can assist you. They can guide you regarding the necessary elements of packaging your CD. Be sure to research and make arrangements to pay royalties and licensing fees for any songs on your CD that are not written by you. ASCAP, BMI and The Harry Fox Agency can answer any questions that you might have on these issues.

In addition to selling CDs, many artists today are selling their songs individually via their websites, as well as on iTunes and other online music sites. This is a great way to make your music available to fans.

Once your CD is packaged and all of the legal aspects have been addressed, you are ready to sell your CDs. You might also want to order other merchandise to round out your merchandise table. Many performing artists sell t-shirts, caps, stickers, key chains, and other pieces of merchandise that fans may want to purchase. There are many companies easily found on the internet that manufacture these types of items.

Performers make money in basically two ways..*live performances* and *merchandise sales.*

Chapter 10

Touring and Merchandising

Touring

Live performances in support of a recording project are referred to as *touring*. Touring can consist of concerts in small venues, medium sized venues, or large venues, depending upon the popularity and draw of the artist. When scheduling a tour it is important to take concert locations into consideration. In order to attract as many people as possible to your concerts, the fans must feel that your concerts are special. The artist must be a controlled commodity. Fans must feel as though this will be their only opportunity to see the artist for a period of time. Scheduling concerts once or twice annually in a particular city is a good tactic. Fans will come out to see an artist that they like year after year. This, of course requires that you have tour stops in many cities. It also requires constant promotion via email, social networking, television, radio, newspapers and every means possible as was discussed earlier in this book.

A concert tour is a series of concerts by a musician or a musical group. These concerts are generally held at a number of venues either in different cities or in different locations. In the Pop, R&B, Country or Rock genres, these concerts can be a series of events that last for weeks, months or even years. Popular artists in these genres are often seen by hundreds of thousands, possibly millions, of fans during the course of their tours. Ticket revenues and merchandise sales are huge as they travel from city to city and often country to country entertaining their fans.

Depending upon the size of the artist's band and crew, touring can mean many things. For example, a cabaret act consisting of a vocalist and an acoustic pianist can travel by car or by plane carrying only their sheet music, sales merchandise, and personal belongings. They would need a maximum of two hotel rooms (unless they were a couple, in which case they would need only one). From this small scenario, we can take a look at a large band like Earth Wind & Fire with more than ten band members and a very large crew. Then there are organizations like the Chicago Symphony Orchestra which consists of more than 100 members in addition to staff and crew that travel with the orchestra. So, as you can see, every touring situation is different and requires a different type of planning.

Many touring artists travel by plane to a particular base area and then use ground transportation to reach tour destinations within a 200 or so mile radius of their base. Other artists use ground transportation for their entire tour. The decision regarding how to travel is almost always based on financial considerations. The whole idea of touring is to make money. The way in which a group travels has a huge impact on the bottom line.

Accommodations also vary. Depending upon the revenue generated by the tour and the expenses to the tour, some artists opt for overnight hotel accommodations, while others sleep in their van or on their tour bus. A business plan and budget should be prepared well in advance of the start of the tour, taking into consideration revenue expectations, and what the projected expenses will be. This will help to assure the financial success of the tour.

The Tour

Before your tour begins, it is important to put together a booklet outlining the tour itinerary. The booklet should be small enough to fit into a pocket or purse, maybe five inches by eight inches so when folded. This size is very manageable. You want the entire crew and all members of the tour to be able to easily carry the itinerary with them all of the time. This minimizes confusion and keeps everyone on track. The itinerary will list each day's activities, including morning bus/van/transportation calls; hotel addresses and distance from concert venue; venue address, phone number and contact person; venue load-in times, show times, sound check times, interview times, contacts, and locations. If you're planning in-store promotional concerts, they should be included on the itinerary as well. It is also good to include which nights you'll be driving out after the show, which nights have hotel stays and which days you'll have off.

Some venues will provide dinner for you before or after the show. This information should be included in the itinerary so that band members know whether or not to eat before reporting to the venue.

A hotel rooming list should also be prepared ahead of time. The information to be included would be the hotel stay date, the hotel name, city, address, and phone number. Band member names, room type, smoking preference and room numbers should also be included on the list. This makes it easy for the hotel and it allows band members to know with whom they will be bunking. It also allows band members to easily find each other while they're staying at the hotel.

Investigate hotel capabilities for equipment storage before your tour begins. Most hotels have a storage area near the front desk. There may be a charge for this service, but it is certainly worth a modest fee to not have the equipment stolen from your vehicle.

Concert Promoter

Concert Tours are often made possible by Concert Promoters or Performing Arts Presenters. Concert Promoters (also known as a Tour promoters or talent buyers) are the individuals or companies responsible for organizing a live concert tour or special event performance. The tour promoter makes an offer of employment to a particular artist, usually through the artist's agent or manager. The promoter and manager (or agent) then negotiate the live performance contract. The majority of live performance contracts are drawn up using the American Federation of Musicians (AFM) standard contract format known as the *AFM Performance Agreement.*

The Concert Promoter's duties include obtaining the performance venue, determining the price for all of the components related to the tour, arranging for and providing transportation for the entire entourage from location to location. The promoter often also pays for advertising (television, radio, newspaper, magazine, etc.). Concert Promoters generally seek corporate sponsorships to raise the money for the tour. The promoter assumes all of the financial risk.

Performing Arts Presenters

A Performing Arts Presenting Organization facilitates exchanges between artists and audiences through performance opportunities. The Performing Arts Presenters utilize artists with prepared presentations. They then match that artist with a venue desiring their type of entertainment. There are several types of presenters that provide entertainment for venues. The venue types are:

Theaters or Concert Halls

Variety of Venue Types (Concert Halls, Festivals, Small Venues, etc.)
Colleges, Universities and Educational Institutions

In addition to these methods of organizing a tour, the manager or artist can organize an independent tour of small and medium-sized venues in different cities. This is where a well-developed facebook, myspace and email list following can be beneficial. The manager should be certain that the artist can sell out the venue before booking. It is important to always give the impression of success. It's better to perform in a small but full venue, rather than a large empty one.

Say for example, an artist has been booked for a concert in Kansas City, perhaps a university or festival date. The artist can seek other performing opportunities at venues 200-to-300 miles from that area. It is important to be considerate of the presenter or promoter sponsoring the Kansas City concert. Another booking too close to their location would most likely impact attendance at their event. As you might image, the presenter or promoter would not be happy with that. As a matter of fact, many promoters and presenters will include a clause in the contract outlining their expectations with regard to other performances in their area for a period of time.

Perhaps that contract would require that the artist not work within a 300-mile radius of the promoter/presenter's venue for 6 months before the event and 3 months after. Or maybe the promoter/presenter would require a full one-year period hiatus in their area before and after the date that they have scheduled with the artist. This is understandable. The promoter/presenter is investing time and resources into the marketing and promotion of the artist's appearance. Naturally they want to generate enough revenue to pay all concert expenses, recoup their investment, and make a profit. As we have already discussed, the artist must be a controlled commodity. The "supply" of the artist's appearances must never exceed the "demand" for the artist. Fans must feel that the artist's appearance is rare and special.

You might ask--well, what about the musicians that work week after week in local bars, restaurants and other small venues in the same town? How are they surviving in the business? The fact is that in many cases, they're just barely surviving in the business. This type of work is generally not very lucrative. It is work offered by small dining and drinking establishments to attract business to those establishments. Musicians across America work in venues like these, in many cases, feeling a great deal of frustration. They are generally not compensated fairly and find themselves stuck in a rut, unable to break away from this type of work. The musician can find regular work in this marketplace, but they are often unfulfilled and underappreciated. The goal of *Music, Money and You--Managing the Business,* is to help musicians find the highest and best use of their musicianship, thereby realizing personal fulfillment and financial success.

Tour Manager

Once the concert tour is booked, a Concert Tour Manager is brought onboard to organize the logistics of the tour. The duties of this individual are budgeting, advancing, and on-the-road.

Budgeting involves determining crew wages, per diem (daily allowance per entourage member), hotel costs, transportation, sound, lighting, work permits, rehearsals, video equipment, other productions costs and other issues.

Advancing involves contacting individual contacts and or venues in each city prior to arrival to ensure that all of the artist's needs will be met. The tour manager will check load-in times and locations, sound check times, and show times. The tour book is compiled with all of this pertinent information and is given to all of the traveling band and crew.

On the Road - The tour manager travels with the band. The tour manager's job on the road varies depending upon the size of the tour, the size of the band, and the level of the artist. On a daily basis, the tour manager is responsible for:

- Overseeing hotel departures on time
- Settling accommodation bills
- Overseeing travel arrangements; i.e. band and crew onto the bus or to the airport in good time
- Paying per diems to band and crew
- Overseeing venue arrival - double-checking hospitality and technical arrangements
- Arranging up-to-date running order with venue and promoter
- Overseeing promotional activities; i.e. TV, radio and press interviews at the venue or at other locations
- Supervising any support or opening acts
- Ensuring venue is ready to open on time by supervising sound check times
- Interacting with the transport department regarding the next days' travel
- Ensuring all acts perform on time and for the allotted time
- Settling performance fee with promoter and collecting any due cash
- Ensuring all touring equipment is re-packed and loaded back onto tour transport
- Preparing band and crew schedule sheets for the next day
- Overseeing band and crew on to appropriate overnight transport or to next hotel
- Reporting this show's attendance figures to management and booking agent

A Concert Tour Manager is a freelancer contracted to work with major acts that have big budgets, large bands/crew and many concert locations. For small or mid-size acts, the Road Manager would perform these duties.

Merchandise Manager

Many artists sell CDs, t-shirts, caps, key chains, mugs and various other pieces of Merchandise while on tour. This can be a huge source of revenue for the artist. The merchandise manager is responsible for handling all things related to the artist's merchandise. This individual, along with the artist and manager, decide what pieces of merchandise would be most appealing to the artist's fan base.

A merchandise manufacturer or wholesaler is identified and the merchandise manager works with the artist's advertising staff to get the graphics that will be used on the merchandise. Based upon the venue sizes and advance ticket sales, the merchandise manager determines what the size of the inventory should be, how many pieces of each item should be ordered, and based on the designation of the artist and the manageró what the pricing for each item type should be. He or she then places the order and waits for the merchandise to arrive. Once the merchandise is in hand, the merchandise manager inventories it utilizing an inventory software program. It is then organized, displayed and made available for purchase at each venue. There is usually one good- sized merchandise kiosk with several sales people for every 500 people attending the event. Wireless credit card machines, secured through a bank or processing company, should be available for credit card purchases.

The merchandise manager oversees the inventory as well as the sales crew. He or she handles all revenue from the sales. He or she completes daily entries into the sales log and reports daily to the tour manager.

Crew

The crew is hired by the Tour Manager or Road Manager. Crew size varies depending upon the size of the tour which means large tours have large crews. For example, in addition to the artist, manager and musicians, for a very successful artist, you might have the following people:

A personal assistant to the featured artist
Production Managers

House sound engineer
Monitor engineers
Audio technicians
Lighting director
Lighting designer
Lighting technicians
Lighting operator
Drum technician
Guitar technician
Keyboard technician
Head of security
Wardrobe person
Bus Drivers
Truck Drivers

The tour or road manager is responsible for managing all of the crew members.

We have taken a general look at the basics of entertainment management. We've covered everything from defining entertainment to reviewing the roles of personnel necessary for a successful entertainment career to tips for recording and touring. Whether you're an artist with a major record deal and lots of money backing you, or an independent artist working small to mid-sized venues, you are surely interested in securing the demand for live music. There is another component of the business that is crucial to the future of live music. We as professional musicians must band together for the sake of live music. Every performer must work to cultivate an audience for intimate live music. During the mid 20th century, there were many small music venues and jazz clubs across America, where one could experience wonderful entertainment. For many reasons, these venues have all but disappeared and the public has become unaccustomed to the concept of what I have dubbed *intimate live music (ILM)*. ILM is music performed in small to mid-sized venues, where the artist and audience share an intimate music experience. "Un-plugged" music of all genres work well in this setting. The entertainer shares information about the music, about the songwriter, or perhaps about him or herself. Not only does the audience get a wonderful entertainment experience, but they leave the venue feeling good about new information learned during the performance. In an effort to preserve live music for future generations, I have developed the "One Hundred People Theory." If practiced by performers, this theory will go a long way toward sustaining and increasing the demand for intimate live music in the 21st Century.

"One Hundred People Theory"

The "One Hundred People Theory" is a very simple concept. It proposes that each professional performer seek to build an audience of One Hundred People, utilizing their personal inner circles, including family, friends, neighbors, colleagues, etc. In addition to building their audience, the performers also constantly tout the value of intimate live music and encourage their following to support other live performing artists as well.

I had an interesting experience during one of my recent performances. I had done the pre-event marketing of the performance via all of the usual methods that I have mentioned in earlier chapters of this book. The 150-seat venue was packed. After the concert, I greeted audience members while signing autographs. A woman and man came to me with tears in their eyes, telling me how much they had enjoyed the concert. They said that they had never experienced anything of that nature before and that they would certainly attend my concerts in the future. I didn't know the man and woman, but they had become fans of live music as a result of that concert. I spoke with them about the power of intimate live music and told them that there are other artists performing around town as well. I encouraged them to make live music a priority when making their entertainment choices.

Their eyes had been opened. So often, in this era of television, recorded music, modern technology and the like, people don't avail themselves of the opportunity to hear live music. People are so accustomed to being inundated with entertainment that insists that bigger is better--louder is better--more is better. This is simply not true. People are realizing that quality is often better that quantity. People are looking for quality experiences that are simple and straight forward. They are deeply moved by the intimate live music experience. It is incumbent upon us as entertainers to reach out to people in our personal spheres and expose them to the beautiful music that we are making. By doing this, we are creating a following for our own music, in addition to creating a following for each other. We are promoting the concept of intimate live music.

This grassroots approach to the longevity of live music is not only good for entertainers in the 21st Century, but it is also good for the small to mid-sized entertainment venues that have all but disappeared over the last 20 years. The *One Hundred People Theory* will make quality entertainment more accessible and more affordable for the public worldwide.

Reach out to the people in your personal sphere. Show them the value of the intimate live music experience. Through our concerted efforts to cultivate the demand for live music, we can create a vehicle for the many talented and skilled musicians that have committed their lives to the study and performance of quality live music.

I wish you much success in charting your own career path. I hope that by utilizing the information provided in *Music, Money & You--Managing the Business,* you will be able to make your dreams come true. Good luck!

Conclusion

To my many friends and colleagues who are struggling in this business as I have struggled in the past--don't lose heart. You are talented and well prepared. You deserve to make a good living with the skills that you have so diligently honed.

As you assimilate and begin to use the information shared within these pages, I would love to hear from you. Let me know how you're using the information and what you're doing to enhance your career.

Thanks so much for taking the time to read *Music Money & You--Managing the Business*. I wish you the very best of luck and I look forward to hearing from you soon. www.gretapope.com

Bibliography

Webster, Noah. "Entertainment." *Webster's Revised Unabridged Dictionary*. 1958.

National Conference of Personal Managers Web Site. Web. 17 May 2010. <http://www.ncopm.com>.(page 27 of dissertation)

Music Business | Music Industry | Record Sales | Billboard Charts | Billboard Hot 100. Web. 17 May 2010. <http://www.billboard.biz>.

EasyBib: Free Bibliography Maker - MLA, APA, Chicago Citation Styles. Web. 17 May 2010. <http://www.easybib.com>.

Waddell, Barnet, and Berry: This Business of Concert Promotion and Touring: A Practical Guide to Creating, Selling, Organizing, and Staging Concerts (Billboard Books, New York, 2007

http://www.tourconcepts.com/tourmanagerdef.html What does a Tour manager do?

Reynolds: The Tour Book (Cengage Learning, Boston, 2007), p 13

http://www.tourconcepts.com/tourmanagerdef.html Tour Concepts

http://www.wikipedia.org

This Business of Artist Management; by Jr. Xavier M. Frascogna (Author), H. Lee Hetherington (Author)

www.ingramcontent.com/pod-product-compliance
Lightning Source LLC
La Vergne TN
LVHW011245080426
835509LV00005B/632